Scottish History

A Captivating Guide to the History of Scotland

Free Bonus from Captivating History (Available for a Limited time)

Hi History Lovers!

Now you have a chance to join our exclusive history list so you can get your first history ebook for free as well as discounts and a potential to get more history books for free! Simply visit the link below to join.

Captivatinghistory.com/ebook

Also, make sure to follow us on:

Twitter: @Captivhistory

Facebook: Captivating History: @captivatinghistory

Contents

Introduction

A sense of poetic irony registers when one learns that Scotland has never won a major military battle when the odds were in their favor.[i] In 1513, the largest Scottish army to ever invade England was defeated by a significantly smaller English army at Flodden Field. In only two hours, the Scots lost 10,000 men. History repeated itself in 1542 when a Scottish army of 15,000 men was defeated by only 3,000 English soldiers. Despite their much smaller numbers, the English managed to take 1,200 Scottish men as prisoners. This humiliating defeat eventually contributed to the demise of King James V.

The massive global success of *Braveheart*, Mel Gibson's Oscar-winning blockbuster epic medieval war film, has helped perpetuate a seductive image of the Scottish as being valiant underdogs, possessors of a brand of earthly pride that serve them well in conflicts with their more powerful southern neighbor. Historical facts do corroborate this impression. When they were pitted against English forces that easily outranked them in numbers and technological sophistication, the Scottish prevailed. William Wallace's victory at the Battle of Stirling Bridge in 1297 is probably the best example of Scottish resilience against the odds. Robert the Bruce has a similar claim to fame with the Battle of Bannockburn seventeen years later when his men defeated an English army that was three times as massive.

England's influence on its northern neighbor after it became the most powerful political force in the British Isles by 1100 cannot be understated. However, Scotland has long insisted on being a separate country on a shared island. Historical facts and myths have been resolutely channeled into the creation of a distinct national identity over the centuries.

For the majority of human history, however, there was no Scotland, Wales, Ireland, or England to speak of.[ii] Scotland is derived from the Latin *Scotia*, which means land of the Scots.[iii] The Scots were a Celtic people of Irish origins who decided to settle on the west coast of Great Britain during the 5th century CE. The people who inhabited Scotia, which only meant the entire kingdom north of England during Alexander II's reign, were certainly not monolingual or monocultural. As the Scottish language slowly became the lingua franca of the entire nation, it had to coexist with Celtic, Gaelic, and Norwegian.

Before a national identity was forged through the trauma of invasion and years of painful resistance, local, regional, and dynastic identities and affiliation had more meaning and relevance to everyone's daily lives. Since roads and advanced technologies for communication did not exist, everyone's existence was rooted in their immediate surroundings. Identities were formed based on the specific physical geography that individuals, families, and clans found themselves in. Scotland's terrain is mostly rugged and subject to weather extremes, but this challenging landscape also possesses a striking beauty and the capacity to facilitate the evolution of a fiercely unique culture.

Scottish folklore has perpetuated the idea that the Scots have "never been conquered." The Scots have certainly fought bravely against conquest from various foreign powers, but they also have a mixed track record. It is true that the Romans eventually abandoned their attempts to conquer Scotland (which was then known as Caledonia) and decided to simply build walls to keep the "barbaric tribes" up north from attacking them. In the 10th century, the Scots managed to fend off a Danish invasion but only with English aid. This dependency meant that the English ruler could define himself as "father and lord" of the King of Scots.

William the Lion (King of Scots from 1165–1214) embodies the potentially large gap between Scotland's reputation for patriotism and nationalism and its more ambiguous historical realities. He may have placed the lion rampant on the Scottish flag, but he also cowered in defeat to the English. After he was captured, he was forced to sign the humiliating Treaty of Falaise in December 1174. This meant that he was only ruling Scotland by the permission of the English crown. After fifteen years, the Scots managed to have the treaty repealed by paying the English a sizable amount of money. (Richard the Lionheart decided to sell off the rights that his father had acquired to finance his ventures in the Holy Land.)

The Treaty of Falaise established the precedent for English monarchs to make claims of overlordship over Scotland. Edward I took advantage of the Scottish succession crisis to assert his dominance over Scotland. His perseverance in conquering Scotland (which earned him the title "the Hammer of the Scots") was nevertheless matched by the Scottish people's refusal to accept English dominion over them. The Scottish nobles, who were initially reluctant to defy Edward I for fears of losing their English lands and titles, were eventually forced to unite in their opposition against England by Robert the Bruce's sacrilegious bid for the throne. Edward's son, Edward II, eventually proved to be an inept military leader who was hopelessly incapable of matching his father's ambitions. When he was defeated at Bannockburn in 1314, Scotland finally reemerged as an independent entity.

In the end, however, Scotland was outmatched by England and its globe-trotting imperial expansionism. The Cromwellian occupation of Scotland in the 1650s achieved the kind of decisive victory that Edward I and his descendants never managed to achieve. Thomas Cromwell's New Model Army followed up its crushing victory at Dunbar in 1650 with their decisive display of military prowess at Worchester in 1651. With 2,000 Scotsmen killed and over 10,000 held as prisoners—along with practically all of the Scottish leaders—Scotland's brave insistence on its independence was finally brought to its knees. Scotland was thus incorporated into the Commonwealth of England. Scotland's independent clergy, parliament, and legal system were no more. The Scots were nevertheless granted 30 seats in the Westminster Parliament (albeit with 15 of them being occupied by English officers).

The Act of Union in 1707 finally achieved James VI's vision of a united Scotland and England. Despite being the first king of Scotland *and* England due to his lineage to both royal lines, he was unable to integrate the two kingdoms during his lifetime. The

Scottish Church, nevertheless, retained its independence, while the Scottish legal system remained separate and distinct from its English counterpart. This arrangement allowed for Scottish economic and intellectual life to flourish, but Scottish fortunes took a downturn as it suffered heavy casualties during the two World Wars.

The recent dominance of the Scottish National Party (SNP), the 2014 Scottish Referendum (on whether Scotland should remain a part of the United Kingdom), and the unfolding bureaucratic complexities of Brexit point toward an incredibly uncertain future. The dilemma that many medieval Scottish monarchs faced—to achieve an alliance with England, its closest neighbor and cultural familiar, or to seek membership with continental Europe—has resurfaced in a modern setting. This time, the wars are to be fought in the court of public opinion, the mass media, and the boardroom instead of on the battlefield.

Chapter 1 – Medieval Strife

To envision what Scotland's earliest history looked like, you must make the effort to consciously imagine a time long before there was a heavily urbanized population. There were no road networks in existence, nor a string of towns and cities connected by frequent trade. The forests were all uncleared, the bogs were filled to the brim, and the heavily mountainous terrain prevented easy migrations up, down, and across the lands. The Highlands (to the north and west), which contained most of Scotland's hills and mountains, were far less hospitable than the flatter and more fertile Lowlands (to the south and east).[iv]

Most long-distance travel and trade would have been achieved by water, along Scotland's ten major rivers, numerous firths, and its extensive coastline. The majority of Scotland's earliest inhabitants toiled in one form of agriculture or another, helping to ensure that their local area could produce all the food and goods it needed to be self-sufficient. One's wealth and happiness largely depended on the fertility of the land that one had access to, as well as one's industriousness in extracting subsistence from it.

The Scottish terrain only became inhabitable to people toward the end of the last glacial period (c. 115,000 to c. 11,700 years ago).[v] Much of North America was blanketed by ice during this time, and the Scandinavian ice sheet extended its reach into the northern British Isles. As the ice made its final retreat northward in approximately 7000 BCE, Mesolithic foragers journeyed northward to access the green pastures it left in its wake. Little is known about the earliest of Scotland's inhabitants since they left little archaeological evidence behind.

A Greek mariner left behind the first written reference to Scotland in about 320 BCE. Pytheas referred to the northern part of the British Isles with the name *Orcas*—a Celtic word that was probably derived from the name of a local tribe he encountered during his travels. It means "the young boars," and it lives on in modern times as Orkney, a rugged archipelago off Scotland's northeastern coast. It also provides evidence that Celtic speakers were present that far up north by the 4th century BCE.

The earliest extensive historical record dates to Rome's first encounter with medieval Scotland. The feared Roman legions arrived toward the end of the 1st century CE after they had successfully conquered the Celtic tribes of England and Wales after three decades of subjugation. Like their southern counterparts, the inhabitants of Scotland (or Caledonia, as the Romans referred to it then) mostly spoke a form of the Celtic language. Unlike southern Britain, however, Caledonia's fierce warrior tribes would mount an effective resistance against the mighty Roman Empire.[vi] Roman ambitions to access Scotland's lead, silver, and gold with plans to enrich itself further by enslaving the Scottish tribes and forcing them to pay taxes would eventually be thwarted.

By the time the Romans first encountered Scotland, a "chiefdom society," which was more hierarchical and unequal, had emerged. Large underground stores (souterrains) were a contributor to this social inequality, allowing local chiefs to hoard surplus crops and resources they had extracted from the land. Hierarchies within Scottish settlements gave way to hierarchies between settlements, as tribes (which each consisted of a few thousand members) vied with each other for power and control over resources.[vii]

In the presence of a foreign common enemy, the warring tribes united to defend their homeland. In 79 CE, the Roman governor led the first incursion into Caledonia.[viii] After a few campaigns, the Romans achieved a decisive victory in 83 CE at the Battle of Mons Graupius. General Julius Agricola defeated the Caledonians there, who were fighting under the leadership of Calgacus, a chieftain of the Caledonian Confederacy. When their initial vision of conquering the entire British Isles was finally at hand, however, the Roman military found that their attention was needed in other parts of their empire.

To safeguard Rome's glorious conquest of southern Britain against the fierce Scottish warriors, the Romans built Hadrian's Wall on the Tyne-Solway line in the 120s and 130s.[ix] During the middle of the 2nd century, a second wall (Antonine Wall) was built on the Forth-Clyde line.[x] This reoccupation only lasted for roughly a decade. After briefly including southern Scotland within the Roman province of Britannia, the Romans eventually gave up their campaign against tribes which were uncharitably described as the "barbarians from the north" and relatively idealized as "the last men on earth, the last of the free." Roman presence was maintained in the southwest part of Scotland, near Hadrian's Wall, until the decline of the Roman Empire.

Despite Rome's aborted conquest of Scotland, its empire left behind a profound influence on the inhabitants of Caledonia. The duality was not entirely between the "imperial Roman" and the "oppressed Native," but between those who were within and outside the mighty empire. The inhabitants of the British Isles had the opportunity to join the Roman army for their own gain, while others undoubtedly saw the benefits of aligning themselves with the most extensive political and social entity in the west.

Like all imperial powers, Rome impacted the locals through a combination of hard and soft power. Apart from their military prowess, they brought Roman commodities, luxury items, and wealth that could be used to seduce local leaders to their cause. The rivaling warrior chiefs were thus incentivized to take advantage of Roman resources to gain a competitive edge over their rivals. When they came face to face with the various trade objects that circulated through Rome's international economic system, the Caledonians inevitably realized that they were isolated from an international highway of ideas, trade, and cultural exchanges.

Rome's most lasting impact on the Caledonians is undoubtedly the introduction of Christianity. The religion of the empire slowly extended its influence up north, reaching places and communities that the Roman military could not. Much of the evangelizing work was probably done by British and Irish missionaries who were intent on converting the northern pagans to their cause. The new religion came with new trade links to the Irish Sea and Atlantic Gaul, which provided the objects necessary for the new Christians to conduct their rituals of faith. This was pottery designed to contain wine and oil, which were inevitably accompanied by new aesthetic and intellectual conceptions.

Chapter 2 - Kenneth MacAlpin, King of the Picts

Five main languages were widely spoken in the territory that is now Scotland in the 9th century. These included three Celtic languages (Briton,[xi] Pict,[xii] and Gael/Scot[xiii]) and two Germanic languages (Angle[xiv] and Norse). It is a historical irony that the most widely spoken language at the time, Pict, was the only one that would eventually become extinct.

Britons and Picts might have shared a common ancestor and originally shared a common language as well, but they began to diverge into two politically and culturally distinct communities by the 8th century. The term "Picti," which means "painted people," was first used by Roman writers as early as the late 3rd century. They were described as enigmatic savage pagans, a tribe that refused to become Romanized or embrace Christianity (as their southern counterparts did). Little remains of their civilization, but there is evidence to suggest that they were not simply primitive warriors. The Picts left behind archaeological evidence of their architecture, art, education, and religion.[xv] They provided no written records for historians to study, but their sophisticated symbols, which can be found on various objects and upright stone monuments, gives off a hint of their burgeoning ethnic and political identity. The lack of any Roman alphabet amongst Pictish relics is especially telling.

The Roman presence intensified the rivalries between the different regional kingdoms vying for power across the land. The various

Germanic tribes that had settled across eastern Britain were beginning to develop a sense of "Englishness," while their counterparts in the west were developing a sense of unity based on their mutual anti-Anglo-Saxon stances. Across the Irish Sea, the various Irish kingdoms were rallying around a shared "Gaelic" identity.[xvi] It is highly likely that the strong regional identities which had persevered in the north during the early medieval period were coalescing into a shared "Pictish" identity due to similar historical factors.

In 400 CE, the Romans made a complete withdrawal from the British Isles as their vaunted empire was increasingly threatened by European tribes. The power vacuum they left behind was soon claimed by the local tribes, who began to exert their control over larger swaths of territories. Despite the Roman exodus, Christianity remained and solidified its presence in Scotland. The kings of Dál Riata (a Gaelic kingdom that extended from Northern Ireland to the west coast of modern Scotland) [xvii] gave Saint Columba—an Irish abbot and missionary who spread Catholicism across the northern British Isles—[xviii] sufficient land to form a monastery in 565 CE. Iona thus emerged as an influential center for Christian learning and evangelism in the Celtic world during the next two centuries.[xix]

The Picts, nevertheless, found themselves confronting another fearsome foreign force throughout the 9th century. The monasteries and the treasures they contained served as a magnet for the Vikings, who sailed across the North Sea to terrorize their southern neighbors and escape the overpopulation on Norway's west coast. [xx] The plunderers seized all the gold and silver (in the form of saintly relics and decorative metalwork) they could find and did not hesitate to murder anyone that stood in the way. Their violent raids eventually gave way to settlements, which allowed them to gain control over large areas of Scotland, Ireland, and England. By the middle of the 9th century, Norse settlements of the western and northern isles and of Caithness and Sutherland were well under way. The image of the peripatetic Viking warrior endures to the modern day, but the truth is that their most important reason for migration was to secure new lands for farming, craftwork, and trade.

The fearsome Viking invasions sowed the seeds of extinction for the once-powerful Pictish kingdom. The Vikings destroyed a monastic settlement at Portmahomack in approximately 820, signaling a decisive change in the status quo. During this period of tumult and confusion, a heroic figure emerged to unite the land against their common seafaring foe.

Kenneth MacAlpin was a Gaelic king who lost his father during an earlier battle with the once-powerful Pictish kingdom. [xxi] MacAlpin took advantage of the crisis to unite the Gaels and Picts against their common foe. There is also evidence to suggest that his mother had been a Pictish princess; his mixed ancestry might have lent a helping hand to the cause (the Pictish were matrilineal, giving him a blood claim to both thrones). A common cultural and political identity was thus forged by the shared need to defend the realm. MacAlpin consolidated his power across the realm by instilling obedience to a single king. As a result, the regional kingdoms across the land lost much of their powers. Instead of regional kings, they became officials who were known as mormaers, or "sea stewards." When the Vikings amassed a fleet of 140 ships to destroy and conquer Dál Riata at the beginning of the 9th century, however, the Gaelic kingdom was brought to an abrupt end. The Gaels relocated the relics of their saints to Pictland (in eastern Scotland) where their presence as Gaelic overlords earned them resentment from the Picts.[xxii]

The union between the Picts and the Scots created Alba, a unified kingdom that spanned across Argyll and Bute to Caithness and included a large majority of central and southern Scotland.[xxiii] Under MacAlpin's leadership, Alba managed to defend itself against the relentless Viking invasions. Despite this victory, the Picts probably had mixed feelings about the new status quo. Gaelic influence, Gaelic Christianity, and Gaelic traditions spread across the former Pictish lands with a greater intensity than ever before. The spread of culture probably occurred in more than one way, as the Gaels intermarried with the Picts and adopted some of their manners and customs. By 839 CE, the Pictish kingdom had been practically annihilated by the Vikings.

When MacAlpin died in 858, his political and historical legacy was clear. The Pictish and Gaelic kingdoms had merged with each other and evolved into the new Kingdom of Alba. Dál Riata disappeared from the chronicles, as did the Picts. The foundation for a Scottish kingdom had been laid down. At his funeral, Gaelic bards mourned his passing: "That Kenneth with his host is no more brings weeping to every home. No king of his worth under heaven is there, to the bounds of Rome."

Chapter 3: Macbeth, the Regicidal King

Macduff: Stands Scotland where it did?

Ross: Alas, poor country! Almost afraid to know itself.

Macbeth, William Shakespeare[xxiv]

The Tragedy of Macbeth stands alongside *Hamlet*, *King Lear*, and *Julius Caesar* as one of William Shakespeare's most enduring tragedies. [xxv] The play was written sometime between 1604 and 1606, over five centuries since the real Scottish king it was based on, Mac Bethad mac Findláich, or Macbeth, was buried.[xxvi] With its prophetic witches, regicide, apparitions of guilt, and a ruthless leading female protagonist (Lady Macbeth), *The Tragedy of Macbeth* has certainly earned a place in literary history.

Despite its iconic fame, however, Shakespeare's play was far from historical truth.[xxvii] The legendary English poet and playwright used the Holinshed's *Chronicles of England, Scotland, and Ireland* (1587) as the primary source for his plot, which was itself riddled in inaccuracies. He also tailored it to fit the tastes of the new reigning English king of his time, King James I. James I had a well-documented interest in witches, witchcraft, and the supernatural—hence the play's opening scene where the Three Witches encounter Macbeth and his friend Banquo. There are various discrepancies between the play and documented historical fact, but modern viewers should especially take note of the fact that Shakespeare took great liberty with the timeline. While the events in the play unfold over the course of a single year, Macbeth remained on the throne of Alba (Scotland did not exist yet) for 17 years.

The well-known murder did happen but not in the way Shakespeare narrated it. Before he assumed the throne, Macbeth succeeded his father, Findlaech, as the chief (or mormaer) of the province of Moray in northern Scotland in 1031. Historians believe that he might have been a grandson of King Kenneth II (reigned 971–995). He married Gruoch (i.e., Lady Macbeth), who was a descendant of King Kenneth III (reigned 997–1005).

Shakespeare paints Macbeth and his wife as ruthless and immoral in their pursuit of political power, but the realities of history are far more complex. Duncan I was the king of Alba from 1034 to 1040,[xxviii] and he had inherited the kingship from his grandfather, King Malcolm II (reigned 1005–1034),[xxix] who had betrayed the established system of royal succession in Alba. The kingship was supposed to be alternated between two different branches of the royal family—a tradition that gave his cousin Macbeth a better claim to the throne.

The rivalry between the two cousins, who each had a rightful claim to the throne through their mothers, culminated in Duncan I's unsuccessful attempt to besiege Durham. The following year, Macbeth murdered him during a battle at Elgin (and not in his bed as he slept, as in Shakespeare's version of events). Macbeth proved to be a respected and wise king who lived on to rule Alba for 17 years. Apart from enforcing law and order across the land, he encouraged his people to embrace Christianity. In 1050, the conditions in Alba were peaceful and secure enough for him to embark on a pilgrimage to Rome.[xxx] Unfortunately for him, history was destined to repeat itself. Duncan's son, Malcolm Canmore,[xxxi] had escaped to Northumbria after his father was defeated and had never intended to give up his claim to the throne. In 1054, his uncle Siward, Earl of Northumbria, challenged Macbeth for the throne on behalf of his nephew. His army defeated Macbeth's at the Battle of Dunsinane.

Macbeth kept the throne but agreed to restore Malcolm's lands to him. Three years later, Malcolm defeated and killed him at the Battle of Lumphanan in Aberdeenshire—this time with help from the English.

Macbeth's life story demonstrates the fragility of medieval kingship throughout this era. A kingship could only be sustained if the king could maintain his political dominance against all his rivals. The system of succession in Alba was tanistry (which is of Celtic origins), which allows a king to be succeeded by any man who had a grandfather who once held the kingship.[xxxii] A man could also lay claim to the throne through a royal mother. When there were multiple claimants (as was often the case), a closer link was advantageous. A council of elders would then collectively decide on which candidate had the strongest claim to the throne. Other attributes (age, wealth, military skill, and personal qualities) were also taken into account. While some early Scottish kings held onto the kingship for decades and died peacefully, many met violent and abrupt ends due to a royal power struggle. Power was thus often secured through the murder of one's predecessor. The contest for kingship largely depended on one's royal standing, access to resources and supporters, and personal ability, rather than ethnicity alone.

Over the years, the northern chiefdom societies evolved to accommodate more intricate structures of government. There was little bureaucracy at this point, but kings began to oversee the law, order, and justice across their lands. With the help of local lords, officials, and legal specialists, they arbitrated disputes and introduced new laws when necessary. Diplomacy was also a crucial concern, as alliances between territories were seldom stable.

Macbeth's embrace and promotion of Christianity also point toward the emerging ideology of a Christian kingship in the north.[xxxiii] It was no longer sufficient for a king to maintain his standing through the use of armed followers and the control of fortified castles and fortresses. Kings began spending more time at influential monasteries, solidifying the interdependence between the once-secular elite classes and the Church. They celebrated major Christian rituals at monasteries they favored and invited leading clerics to participate in crucial royal ceremonies. Both parties were invested in maintaining stability, peace, and a strong leadership that could stand the test of time.

Chapter 4 – The Emergence of the Scottish Nation-State

During Macbeth's relatively long and peaceful reign, southerners who were loyal to him migrated northward, opting to resettle in the southwest and northeast of modern-day Scotland. They brought with them a more international outlook and culture, sowing the seeds of foreign influence in a predominantly Gaelic society. Gaelic traditions and customs prevailed in everyday life, the Church, and the royal courts, as well as the institutions of law and education. This was set to change throughout the 11th and 12th centuries, though.

The rising presence of foreign influences in the north can be traced back to Malcolm Canmore who became the King of Alba as Malcolm III in 1058 (after Macbeth's death the previous year). His first wife, Ingibjorg, was the daughter of the Norse Earl of Orkney, but his second wife, Margaret,[xxxiv] was a descendant of England's Saxon royal house. As a queen consort and patroness of the Church, Margaret ushered in a receptive climate to southern cultural influences (i.e., the Anglicization of Scotland). By influencing her husband and his court, she advanced the causes of the Gregorian reform (which was mainly preoccupied with the clergy's independence from the state) and the conquered English population.

Margaret also relocated Benedictine monks from Canterbury, England, to her new foundation at Dunfermline, establishing the precedent for non-Gaelic-speaking clergymen to influence Scottish culture.

When Malcolm III died during his final English raid in 1093, however, there were concerted attempts to prevent the replacement of tanistry with primogeniture.[xxxv] This southern custom privileged the legitimate firstborn son above everyone else (younger brothers, older or younger illegitimate sons, and collateral relatives) when it came to inheriting his parent's throne, estate, or wealth. Under tanistry, the heir to the king *could* be the eldest son, but this was not necessarily the case. A council of family heads could opt to elect a brother, nephew, or cousin of the previous chieftain—anyone who was linked by blood and deemed most worthy of the position.

Malcolm III's brother and son (from his first marriage) each briefly occupied the throne after his death. In time, however, it was Malcolm III's three sons, with the assistance of Margaret, who secured their control over the throne. Edgar was king from 1097–1107, followed by Alexander I (1107–24) and David I (1124–53). With the help of the English, they defied Celtic opposition and claims from the descendants of their father's first marriage. Their rise to power was accompanied by the increasing practice of primogeniture, which finally replaced tanistry permanently during the late 13th century.

The presence of Latin in Scotland had linked it to the international culture of the Christian Church over the previous decades, which paved the way for the impact of other influences from continental Europe. Throughout the 12th and 13th centuries, the "Europeanization of Europe" was under way, as the modern Western European state began developing in England, France, Norway, and Germany. They were categorized by clearly defined borders, national sovereignty, a commercial economy, parliamentary representation, thoroughly institutionalized administrative and legal systems, and a shared idea of nationhood. The arrival of immigrants from Normandy, Brittany, and Flanders accelerated the disruption of Gaelic norms and traditions, bringing in new influences, ideas, and practices that could be repurposed for Scottish ends.

David I, the youngest of Malcolm III's six sons with Margaret, played a major role in Scotland's evolution into a modern nation-state.[xxxvi] He eventually proved himself to be one of the most powerful and influential Scottish kings. Unlike his mother, who did not interfere much with the inner workings of the Church, he actively reorganized Scottish Christianity to align it with its counterparts in England and continental Europe. This meant that there was a clear division between the secular and regular clergy, as well as a complete system of parishes and dioceses. He also founded several religious communities, mainly for Cistercian monks and Augustinian canons.

On the political front, David I introduced an Anglo-French (Norman) aristocracy that would go on to play a significant role in Scottish history.[xxxvii] Much of his early life had been spent at the court of his brother-in-law, King Henry I of England. Like his father before him, his marriage to a prominent Englishwoman (a daughter of Waltheof, Earl of Northumbria) earned him significant political clout in England. Through his wife, he became the Earl of Huntingdon, a title that came with large swaths of land in Northamptonshire. His Anglo-Norman connections helped him secure the right to rule Cumbria, Strathclyde, and part of Lothian before he succeeded the throne after his older brother, Alexander I.[xxxviii]

Despite his English connections, David I remained an independent king who was intent on drawing from English culture and bureaucracy to empower Scotland.[xxxix] He paved the way for other Anglo-Norman families to migrate northward by providing generous rewards of offices and lands. These included the Bruces in Annandale, the Fitzalans of Arundel, and the de Morvilles in Ayrshire. They were given control of large estates in peripheral areas where David I's regal authority could not be easily enforced.

This decentralized form of government thus introduced a form of feudalism in Scotland.[xl] A four-tier hierarchy developed, with the king at the apex followed by the nobles, knights, and serfs. The nobles possessed lands from the Crown for their military services, which were provided through the training and recruitment of knights. These knights also protected the peasants on their lord's lands, who provided their labor and a share of their crops in exchange for this protection. Similar feudal arrangements had existed amongst the clan systems of the Scottish Highlands, but these were mainly based on family bonds instead of written charters and legal contracts.

David I's rule over the Scottish kingdom was also consolidated through the creation of a more sophisticated government administration. He introduced the offices of sheriff (vicecomes), a royal judge, and an administrator for each area of the kingdom. Central government officials such as the chancellor, the chamberlain, and the justiciar were introduced to the royal court. The royal court also began establishing itself as the supreme court of law and parliament, maintaining an efficient government that facilitated peace and the flourishing of a medieval economy and society.

There are four main characteristics which clearly differentiated David I's kingship from the traditional Celtic-style kingship that his predecessors had practiced.[xli] Firstly, David I extended royal power into practically every aspect of life (mainly the religious and the economic). He reformed the Scottish Church and extended its religious orders across the land while also introducing an English-type market economy. This included the introduction of formal markets and fairs that required trading licenses that were administered by the Crown. David I also minted the first Scottish coinage and founded the kingdom's four royal burghs (Berwick, Edinburgh, Perth, and Aberdeen). His trusted nobles established firm local lordships centered on well-defended castles. They also sent their knights to serve in his army, which allowed him to experiment with the various tools and policies of an English-style administrative kingship.

Secondly, he established a more totalizing and monopolistic royal lordship across a "greater Scotland"—a tradition that greatly benefited his successors. The older tradition of tanistry—which nearly always engendered great chaos and uncertainty—was abandoned in favor of a stricter order for the royal succession. This left the regional kings with little opportunity to compete for the throne as succession was now a matter of direct lineage. True to his centralizing ambitions, David preemptively elected his only son Henry as a co-ruler in 1135. After Henry's unexpected early demise in 1152, David appointed his oldest grandson as his apparent heir. Malcolm IV thus became king in 1153 at the previously implausible age of 12 when his grandfather died (a regent nevertheless safeguarded the throne until he was old enough to rule on his own).[xlii] A strict adherence to primogeniture thus helped to spare the Scottish kingdom from disruptive upheavals and violent competition for the throne.

Thirdly, David I and his government sought to empower the Scottish kingship to be on equal footing with the English kingship. The objective was to thwart the English monarchy's imperial aspirations and to foster a greater sense of identity and status as a decidedly independent kingdom. The Scottish Church thus lobbied the pope for papal approval of the Scottish kingship, an effort that was thwarted until 1329 by rigorous English lobbying. This concept of a "divine" and "semi-sacred" kingship was also a potent means for David I to consolidate his rule. In the meantime, the Scottish Church insisted on remaining independent from the influence of its counterparts in Canterbury or York.

Finally, the Scottish kings began to seek a stronger footing on an international stage. They embraced European courtly fashions and began participating in international diplomacy. David I succeeded in winning respect and admiration from his continental European peers—the first Scottish monarch to do so. He even envisioned himself as a potential leader of the Second Crusade. His court embraced English and French (which were both the lingua franca of political society) to such an extent that an Englishman commented that the Scots "regarded themselves as…Frenchmen in race, manners, language, and culture."[xliii] Scottish princesses began marrying continental princes with greater frequency, while their male counterparts married English, French, and Norwegian princesses or high-born women. From here on, the Scottish kings insisted on being viewed as equals to the Western European monarchs.

Chapter 5 – The Golden Age

David I's modernizing reign lasted for nearly three decades, from 1124 to 1153. By the time he died and was replaced by his grandson Malcolm IV, his lands had sprawled forth to include Newcastle and Carlisle. His wealth and power rivaled the king of England, which undoubtedly helped him to maintain his mythical status as a saintly and powerful ruler throughout the land. The Scottish kings who followed suit may not have matched the immensity of his achievements, but they built on his legacy in their own ways. The inhabitants of Scotland thus enjoyed an unprecedented period of prolonged peace and prosperity from David I (reigned 1124–1153) to Alexander III (reigned 1249–1286).

The Scottish economy flourished for over a century due to innovation and progress. A predominantly agrarian economy gave way to urbanization, and the burghs (incorporated towns) bustled as hubs for trade and small-scale manufacturing. David I helped facilitate the evolution of towns in Edinburgh, Dunfermline, Perth, Stirling, Inverness, and Aberdeen by encouraging intranational and international trade, introducing a robust legal system, and providing security against attacks from pirates and mercenaries. Each burgh was also allowed to develop their own laws to regulate trading transactions and resolve disputes. If a local burgh was unable to resolve a dispute, it could be referred to the Court of the Four Burghs (which initially included Berwick, Edinburgh, Roxburgh, and Stirling).

Berwick[xliv] may not rival the international reputations of Glasgow[xlv] and Edinburgh[xlvi] (the state capital, now and then) today, but it was *the* epicenter for Scottish economic activity during this time. Despite David I's English ties, Scotland counted northern Germany and Scandinavia as its primary trading partners during the 12ᵗʰ and 13ᵗʰ centuries. Despite being home to only half a million people (for comparison, England had approximately 2 million people), Scottish farmers produced more wool and cattle than their English counterparts. They also had the benefit of low taxation, access to ample amounts of food and wine, and the luxury of plying their trade along a good transportation network. Many of the original townspeople were actually relative newcomers to Scotland, eager for a chance to focus on their economic activities instead of struggling to survive in locales plagued by territorial disputes and never-ending medieval warfare.

Medieval visitors to Berwick compared it to Alexandria, Egypt, for its wealth and sizable population. The stereotypes of the Scots as a barbaric and tribal people were not evident here. Indeed, Berwick's annual customs revenue alone was estimated to amount to 25 percent of England's as a whole. The presence of well-endowed monasteries, stately abbeys, and grand churches reflected the strong and genteel influence of Christianity over all aspects of life. Its presence as a unifying religion undoubtedly helped to maintain the peace and harmony between the multicultural communities that lived in close proximity to one another. Political conflicts often disrupted the general peace and stability that David I's successors enjoyed, but it did not have a major impact on the economy. David I's grandson Malcolm IV did not match his grandfather's cult of personality or reputation, but he was nevertheless a relatively successful king. He never married and had a reputation for chastity (this earned him the unflattering nickname "the Maiden"). He did decide to surrender Cumbria and Northumbria to Henry II to build better relations with England, but he also was successful in defeating Somerled.ˣˡᵛⁱⁱ Somerled was a powerful "King of the Isles," a regional ruler that reigned in the Western Isles of Scotland which were primarily allied to the Norwegian kingdom. He had ambitions to make the islands an entirely independent kingdom and was victorious against the Scandinavians in Argyll. His aim to include parts of the mainland into his territory ultimately sealed his violent death at the hands of his own nephew, William I.

William I succeeded Malcolm IV in 1165 and shared David I's

expansionist objectives.[xlviii] He earned the nickname "William the Lion" for successfully subduing the north (across the Moray Firth) and building royal castles there. His plans to reclaim Northumbria from the English unfortunately resulted in humiliation. During a failed raid into England, he was captured by Henry II's men. In exchange for his release, he and other Scottish nobles agreed to acknowledge Henry II as their feudal overlord via the Treaty of Falaise (1174). As a result, English garrisons were placed all over Scotland. William was able to redeem himself in 1189 when he negotiated for the Treaty of Falaise to be annulled in exchange for a hefty payment of 10,000 marks via the Quitclaim of Canterbury (1189).

English kings could, nevertheless, still advance more ambiguous claims of superiority over Scotland, as they had throughout the previous century. Thankfully, William the Lion's successors were competent kings who succeeded in maintaining the peace, power, and prosperity that David I had attained. William's son, Alexander II, (reigned 1214–1249) secured a lasting peace between Scotland and England with the Anglo-Scottish agreement of 1217.[xlix] This mutual commitment was strengthened by his marriage to Henry III's sister Joan in 1221. This meant that the longstanding ambition to claim Northumbria as part of Scotland had to be renounced, however. The border between England and Scotland was thus established by the Tweed-Solway line after centuries of indeterminacy.

Alexander III (reigned 1249–1286) followed his father's choice of a politically strategic marriage.[l] In 1251, he married Henry III's daughter Margaret. He proved to be a wise and beloved king who expanded the kingdom with the acquisition of the Western Highlands and Isles after the Battle of Largs (which is also known as the Last Battle of the Vikings) in 1263.[li] King Haakon Haakonsson's catastrophic defeat marked the end of Viking influence over Scotland.[lii] When Alexander III met an abrupt and unexpected end in 1286, however, the integrity of his own kingdom was severely threatened. With his death, Scotland's long and cherished golden age came to an end.

Chapter 6 – The Wars of Independence

Alexander III's two sons had died before him in 1281 and 1284. In hopes of a male heir, he married a young French noblewoman, Joleta of Dreux. (His first wife, Princess Margaret of England, had died in 1275.) Despite a dire prophecy of his impending doom by Thomas the Rhymer, the famous prophet, he decided to ride home to his castle at night during a treacherous storm. After losing contact with his guides and squire, he and his horse were found dead at the bottom of a cliff the next morning.

All hope was technically not lost, as Alexander III had arranged for his young granddaughter Margaret (the "Maid of Norway") to assume the Scottish throne.[liii] The appointed guardians of Scotland arranged for her hand in marriage with Lord Edward (King Edward I's then five-year-old son) via the Treaty of Birgham (1290) in hopes of maintaining the peace between Scotland and England.[liv] When Margaret died due to seasickness while sailing from Norway to Scotland four years later, however, the longstanding Scottish monarchy had come to an untimely end.

After Margaret's death, no less than 13 claimants for the Scottish crown revealed their plans for the throne. The majority of these were Scottish magnates. The guardians made the costly mistake of inviting Edward I to serve as an external arbitrator for these claims. Edward I, who had already proven his appetite and aptitude for expansion and conquest with the dominion of Ireland and Wales, did not waste any time in making full use of the power void. Instead of being an impartial judge, he opted to assert his position as Scotland's feudal superior. The claimants to the throne were in a poor position to oppose Edward I, as were the various members of the Scottish nobility who held precious land titles in England.

The common people of Scotland (i.e., the "community of the realm") and the Scottish clergy were, nevertheless, deeply opposed to the idea of English dominion. Edward I's heavy-handed attempt to assimilate Scotland into England ultimately prompted the rise of a powerful sense of national unity that rose from the grassroots to the upper echelons of the Scottish social hierarchy. Their antagonism to the English presence in everyday life and through the unwanted interference from the English Church would engender a nationalism that cut across barriers of religion, class, ethnicity, and language. This hard-won national consciousness certainly did not emerge overnight. Edward I was initially able to extend his dominion over Scotland—maintaining it was what ultimately proved to be untenable.

The two main candidates for the throne were John de Balliol[lv] and Robert de Bruce.[lvi] Both men had many supporters and armed forces at their command. Edward I had a logical reason to choose John Balliol over Robert the Bruce, but it was also in his favor that the former possessed large swaths of land in northern England. He had far more to lose if he chose to defy his self-appointed English overlord.

Balliol did endure a series of humiliations as Edward I unsubtly exerted his overlordship. He made every Scottish magnate, knight, freedman, and religious leader swear their loyalty to him (as Lord Paramount of Scotland) or risk harsh penalties. Edward also made Balliol repeat his homage to him multiple times in front of all the other Scottish nobles. Balliol's resentment at being blatantly reduced to a puppet figure grew. When Edward took it a step further and had English judges preside over law cases that were being appealed in Scottish courts and demanded that Balliol send his knights to perform military service for the English war with France, a full-fledged rebellion was sparked.

In 1295, the Scottish established an alliance with France in their opposition to England. The historic Auld Alliance was primarily motivated by Scotland and France's mutual interest in curtailing England's expansionary ambitions. While it was primarily intended to be a military and diplomatic alliance, it also had long-lasting cultural effects on Scotland. It granted Scottish merchants the opportunity to gain the first choice in importing Bordeaux's finest wines—a privilege that the Scots held onto for centuries. Scottish appetites for French wines persisted even in the face of the Reformation, which created an irreconcilable rift between Catholic France and Protestant Scotland.

In response to Scotland's rekindled alliance with France, Edward I ordered his army to annihilate Berwick. He also ordered for all of Balliol's English titles and properties to be confiscated. His army of 3,000 foot soldiers and 5,000 horsemen wreaked havoc on Scotland's prized city to deter the Scottish resistance. Out of a population of approximately 20,000 people, only 3,000 survived the massacre and pillage. The Scottish persevered, but they were no match for the most sophisticated military force in all of Europe. Edward I eventually captured no less than 130 high-ranking Scottish knights, as well as several earls and prominent magnates. After he seized control of all major Scottish castles—Roxburgh Castle, Edinburgh Castle, and Stirling Castle—there was no option but to surrender.

Balliol was shipped off to England and placed under house arrest. The Scottish nobility had lost their will to resist English subjugation by now, leaving William Wallace—a knight's son with no lands or prestige to his name—to emerge as an iconic embodiment of the Scottish desire for independence.[lvii] After a series of skirmishes against the obnoxious English knights and officials that made life difficult for the Scottish common people, Wallace evolved from a rebel outlaw into an ingenious guerrilla leader.

Tales of his heroic exploits (which mirrored the English legend of Robin Hood) and his ascendance to near-mythical status (a Christ-like resurrection from the dead and a prophecy of national heroism) attracted followers and allies across the land. In 1297, Wallace made full use of an advantageous terrain and English military overconfidence to land an astounding victory at the Battle of Stirling Bridge. This was Scotland's most significant victory against the English army since the Dark Ages. Wallace's newfound power and fame as a national hero and military genius were nevertheless short-lived. During the Battle of Falkirk the following year,[lviii] he suffered a devastating defeat. He died via a gory execution in London in 1305, partly because his lowly social status had triggered envy, resentment, and opposition from many members of the Scottish nobility. Without their united support, Wallace's army of rebels could not hold out against Edward I's military might for long.

Wallace's excruciating death was not in vain, though. In his place, a royal rebel rose to forcefully unite the Scottish nobility to resist the "Hammer of the Scots." The eighth Robert de Bruce, the grandson of Balliol's main competitor for the throne, ultimately staged an unexpected revolt in 1306. Like Wallace before him, Bruce realized that his only opportunity to best the more numerous and technologically advanced English army was by relying on ambushes, guerrilla tactics, surprise attacks, and unconventional military strategies.[lix] After suffering from a series of agonizing defeats (and enduring the executions of many of his family members), Bruce turned the tables and achieved a series of career-making victories against the English: the Battle of Glen Trool in 1307,[lx] the Battle of Loudoun Hill that same year,[lxi] and the historic Battle of Bannockburn in 1314 (where his men defeated the largest English army to ever invade Scotland).[lxii]

Robert the Bruce proved himself as a skillful statesman and military leader, excelling both at harrying Edward I's attempts to subjugate him and at firmly suppressing his local opponents. When Edward I finally died in 1307—while journeying to the Scottish front lines, no less—Bruce was able to take advantage of his successor Edward II's weaknesses to negotiate for Scottish independence.

In 1320, he put forth the Declaration of Arbroath with the help of his advisers. It was framed as a letter from the Scottish magnates to the pope, announcing their allegiance to Bruce as the rightful king of Scotland. It also sought the Roman Church's support for Scotland as an independent kingdom from England and to reverse the pope's excommunication of Bruce (he had risen to power by murdering a rival for the throne in a church). In October 1328, Pope John XXII finally lifted Bruce's excommunication.

It was Edward II's hopeless incompetence and local enemies that eventually helped Bruce secure the English recognition of Scotland's independence. Edward II was deposed from power by his own wife,

Princess Isabella of France, with the help of her lover, exiled English baron Roger Mortimer. She replaced him with their young son Edward III, who was in a highly vulnerable position and ill-equipped to maintain a war against Scotland while also having to suppress the rebellious English nobles.

The Treaty of Edinburgh-Northampton was signed by Edward III (under pressure from his mother and Mortimer) and Bruce in 1328.[lxiii] It dictated that he renounced all claims of overlordship over the kingdom of Scotland, sought to maintain the peace between the two kingdoms via the arranged marriage between Bruce's son David and Edward III's sister Joan, and officially recognized Bruce as the rightful King of the Scots. Bruce himself died the following year, having sealed his place in Scottish history. The traditions that had been established during the long and torturous Wars of Independence—to pursue self-sufficiency despite the high costs incurred and to turn toward continental Europe for inspiration and alliances—would persist until the 16th century.

Both William Wallace and Robert the Bruce enjoy a seemingly immortal place in the hearts and minds of subsequent generations of Scottish men and women. Wallace's status as a patriot of the first order endures via an epic poem by 15th-century Scottish royal court poet Harry the Minstrel (or "Blind Harry").[lxiv] *The Actes and Deidis of the Illustre and Vallyeant Campioun Schir William Wallace* (Acts and Deeds of the Illustrious and Valiant Champion Sir William Wallace) enshrined Wallace's mythical status over the centuries, which then reached a global audience via Mel Gibson's 1995 blockbuster Oscar-winning film *Braveheart*.[lxv] Bruce is less well known outside of Scotland, but his contributions to the nation are similarly preserved for posterity via John Barbour's 14th-century poem *The Bruce*—the first major work of Scottish literature.[lxvi]

Chapter 7 – The Black Death

Historians tend to focus on human actions and consequences when attempting to reconstruct the past. The pages of history are filled with the lives of kings, popes, powerful human institutions, wars, battles, and periods of significant cultural changes like the Reformation and Industrial Revolution. Numbers tend to be freer from such biases. The Scottish casualties from the many battles and skirmishes with the English military throughout the Scottish Wars of Independence were certainly significant. However, the catastrophic impact of the Black Death on Scotland cannot be ignored.[lxvii]

After killing millions as it spread westward from China and throughout the Mediterranean, the Black Death devastated England between 1348 and 1349. Deaths were caused by a combination of fatal airborne diseases: the bubonic plague (during the summer months), the pneumonic plague (during winter), and possibly anthrax. Modern scientific studies attribute the infection to the bacterium *Yersinia pestis* (this strain is ancestral to all currently existing *Y. pestis* strains), but there is also evidence to indicate that it may have had viral origins. The inhabitants of medieval Europe believed that the plague was airborne, but scientists believe that it actually spread on the backs of rodents (primarily rats) who were surreptitiously infested with plague-carrying fleas.

London was hit in September 1348 with the entirety of East Anglia affected the following year. Wales and the Midlands were infected by the spring of 1349. That summer, it spread across the Irish Sea and penetrated northward into Scotland. Historians believe that the Scots had been infected because they chose to attack various English towns as they were succumbing to the plague. Believing that the disease was retribution from God, nearly 5,000 Scottish soldiers fielded a botched attempt to invade England.

Scotland did not suffer as much as its Western European counterparts because of its cooler climate and more dispersed population. Even so, the plague was capable of wiping out the majority of the urban populations based in cities like Glasgow and Edinburgh. An English account of the pandemic reveals that even small villages were not fully spared from its deadly embrace:

> Sometimes it came by road, passing from village to village, sometimes by river, as in the East Midlands, or by ship, from the Low Countries or from other infected areas. On the vills of the bishop of Worcester's estates in the West Midlands, they (the death rates) ranged between 19 per cent of manorial tenants at Hartlebury and Hanbury to no less than 80 per cent at Aston…It is very difficult for us to imagine the impact of plague on these small rural communities, where a village might have no more than 400 or 500 inhabitants. Few settlements were totally depopulated, but in most others whole families must have been wiped out, and few can have been spared some loss, since the plague killed indiscriminately, striking at rich and poor alike.

"The World Upside Down," in *Black Death in England*, J. Bolton[lxviii]

Apart from the mystery of its origins and how it spread, the Black Death was so terrifying because of the speed in which it struck and the scale of its activity. Entire villages could be wiped out in a matter of days, while large urban areas could easily lose between eighty to ninety percent of their populations. The exact number of Scottish people that died due to the plague is unknown, but historians estimate that about a fifth of Scotland's population was lost during this time (approximately one million people). Even this conservative estimate is enough to make it the most fatal calamity in the history of the kingdom.[lxix] The very small minority who survived an infection had to live the rest of their lives with crippling mental and physical disabilities.

The first signs that someone had been infected was usually the emergence of lumps in the armpits or groin. After that, angry black spots began to appear on the thighs, arms, and other parts of the body. This was typically a death sentence within three days. The colder Scottish climate deterred the bubonic form of the plague, but it allowed the pneumonic and septicaemic plague to achieve a high death toll. The nobles were often spared by virtue of their isolation in the castles, but the middle and lower classes were mostly unable to escape its ravages.

To make matter worse, the plague was not a one-off phenomenon. Instead, it returned to haunt Scotland multiple times throughout the subsequent centuries (the final outbreak occurred in the 1640s). It stifled all aspects of life, from the economic to the political to the cultural. Children whose parents were dying from the plague refused to visit their deathbeds out of fear of becoming infected themselves. There was a shortage of labor, leaving many farms unmanned for years. Many fields were allowed to rot, reversing all of the agricultural and manufacturing progress that had been achieved after the Wars of Independence finally came to an end. Wars were halted, as did much of intranational and international trade.

Combating the plague certainly took its toll on Scotland. In the 17th century, it finally managed to return to pre-plague population levels. This was achieved by the implementation of strict health controls whenever an outbreak occurred. People were prohibited from gathering, and those believed to be infected were placed in quarantine. The Foul Clengers were widely employed in Edinburgh and other Scottish towns by this time. Their job was to relocate plague victims far away from human settlements to die and to burn all their homes, clothes, and possessions to the ground.

Chapter 8 – The House of Stewart

The Scottish economy recovered from the massive outbreak of plague by the 1370s. The exports of wool reached new heights, providing ample profits that ensured that the Scottish survivors of the plague had access to plenty of meat. This newfound prosperity also coincided with a new political development.

David II had succeeded his father Robert the Bruce in 1329 when he was only five years old.[lxx] By the time of David's death in 1371, Scotland still maintained the independence his father had fought so valiantly for. Like his father, David II had been fairly successful in suppressing local opposition to the throne. The main threats to his power came from competing claims for the throne from John Balliol's descendants and hostility from the "disinherited" landowners who had been stripped of their titles by his father for supporting the English during the Wars of Independence. The war with England had been replaced by trade, allowing his citizens to enjoy the peace while his government used the taxes they collected to rebuild the kingdom. These taxes were also used to pay David II's ransom to England (100,000 marks), which had been incurred after he was captured during his attempt to invade England in 1346.

When he died unexpectedly, David II had been in the process of divorcing his second wife to marry his most recent mistress. This personal tumult was undoubtedly motivated by the urgency to produce an heir. David II had hoped for Edward III of England or one of his sons to assume the throne after he died, but this was an abominable prospect to the community of the realm who had endured years of hardship to retain their independence.

David II's manner of kingship and the Bruce dynasty were thus effectively buried with him. An entirely new dynasty emerged to fill the void—the House of Stewart (which is also spelled as "Stuart" and "Steuart."[lxxi] David II was succeeded by Robert II, who had been serving as the high steward of Scotland during David II's prolonged captivity.[lxxii] He was the son of Marjory (Robert the Bruce's daughter) and Walter Stewart. Robert II was a fairly ineffectual and incompetent ruler, but he was an overachiever in the one domain that the Bruces had failed at. He fathered at least 21 children (with two wives and several mistresses) within his lifetime.

This surprisingly large number of offspring points toward Stewart's new model of kingship. Instead of a lone monarch exerting his power throughout the realm, Robert II was intent on elevating the size, status, and reach of his entire familial network. He married off his daughters to the Lord of the Isles, the Earl of Douglas, and other Scottish magnates. His sons were responsible for no less than eight earldoms and the duties of principal lieutenants. He bequeathed extended family members with patronage and empowered them to oversee distant regions.

This dynastic model of kingship had its advantages and disadvantages. On the one hand, the sharing and spreading of power helped maintain political stability. When members of the royal family began competing overtly for power, however, that stability proved to be highly fragile. Bitter family feuds reared their ugly heads as Robert II was removed from active rule by his own son, the Earl of Carrick. In 1388, he himself was ousted from his self-assumed lieutenant position by his younger brother, Robert of Fife.

These events were a precedent for a new development: The king could be stripped of his duties in favor of lieutenants who had wider support. After over a hundred years of continuous monarchical rule, active kingship became an increasingly rare phenomenon. The kings from the House of Stewart were largely ineffectual and unreliable, leaving their lieutenants to assume control over important matters like war and justice. Guardians and governors also began to enjoy a newfound significance.

The Stewart kings were not without their own accomplishments, but they failed to rival the glory of the previous generation of monarchs. In one way or another, they left behind a legacy that left something to be desired: (1) Robert III (reigned 1390-1406)[lxxiii] was unable to prevent the English from capturing his own son; (2) James I (reigned 1406–1437)[lxxiv] spent most of his time as king raising taxes and confiscating lands from the Scottish nobility to pay off his English ransom; (3) James II (reigned 1437–1460)[lxxv] assumed the throne after his father was murdered and assumed a penchant for warfare—he was killed by his own siege gun while besieging Roxburgh Castle; (4) James III (reigned 1460–1488)[lxxvi] was killed while attempting to escape the Battle of Sauchieburn in Stirlingshire.

The weakness of the Crown thus encouraged a more regionalized form of politics to take shape. Despite the king's reduced status and the limited influence of the royal government, the idea of a unified Scottish realm persisted. The king's symbolic power increased as his actual power diminished, partly due to epic poems like John Barbour's *The Bruce*, which signaled the emergence of a national body of literature. The Scottish Church and institutions of learning (e.g., the newly founded University of St. Andrews) also helped to ensure that the idea of an independent Scotland remains viable and attractive to all its inhabitants.

Founded in 1413, the University of St. Andrews was Scotland's first university and an entirely necessary development since Scotland could no longer send its students (who were often studying to become part of the clergy) to Paris. The Wars of Independence had prompted them to study in Paris instead of Cambridge or Oxford. But when Scotland opted to recognize the antipope Benedict XIII after France abandoned him, a local alternative was needed.[lxxvii] The Great Western Schism (1378 to 1417)—which involved intense internal divisions caused by the advent of three rival popes within the Roman Catholic Church—thus played an unintended role of catalyzing the birth of Scotland's own institutions of higher education.[lxxviii] In 1451, Bishop William Turnbull founded the University of Glasgow, Scotland's second university.[lxxix]

Chapter 9 – Mary, Queen of Scots: "The Daughter of Debate"

After a series of lackluster Stewart kingships, James IV assumed the throne as a 15-year-old in 1488.[lxxx] Despite his young age, he proved to be adept at matters of war, politics, and culture. His primary achievements include the downfall of the last Lord of the Isles, the founding of King's College (Scotland's third university) and improvements in education, and the great age of Scottish poetry. He also resolved the unrest along the Anglo-Scottish border and achieved a "treaty of perpetual peace" with England, which was sealed through his marriage with Henry VII's daughter Margaret Tudor in 1503.

Unfortunately, this peace proved to be far from perpetual. Henry VIII became complicit in Pope Julius II's anti-French campaign during the Italian Wars (1494 to 1559), prompting Scotland to renew its anti-England alliance with France.[lxxxi] During this time, the French king, Charles VIII, made several attempts to invade Italy with the help of Spain. To defend Rome, the papacy formed an alliance with Henry VIII, Venice, and Florence in 1526. James IV responded to Henry VIII's French invasion by mounting a rash offensive against England. After successfully capturing four castles in northern England in August 1513, he suffered from a calamitous defeat. He perished, along with thousands of Scottish soldiers, at the disastrous Battle of Flodden.

His successor James V (reigned 1513–42) worked to offset the extravagant costs of his predecessor's international aspirations.[lxxxii] Apart from having to deal with the hefty royal debts he had inherited (for artillery, a large navy, and embassies abroad), he also had to manage the divisions between French Catholic supporters and those who wanted Scotland to adopt a more financially prudent stance of neutrality. James V's two successive French marriages indicated where his loyalties lay. His support for France and the papacy cost him valuable support from the Scottish nobility (especially the Protestants), as did his penchant for extracting wealth to finance his campaigns.

Their apathy for the king proved to be fatal when Henry VIII attacked Scotland in 1542. After his small army was routed near the border at Solway Moss in 1542, James V suffered from a fatal mental breakdown. His legitimate infant sons had perished (possibly due to nervous prostration), leaving behind one surviving female legitimate child: Mary Stuart (Mary, Queen of Scots).[lxxxiii]

Born a mere week after her father's death, Mary was eventually shipped off to France for protection at the age of five by her mother, Mary of Guise.[lxxxiv] In her absence, Mary of Guise served as acting regent after fending off Henry VIII's attempt to control his great-niece. Mary had a sheltered and privileged upbringing at the court of King Henry II and Queen Catherine de' Medici where her welfare was overseen by her mother's influential relatives. She hunted, danced, learned a variety of languages including Latin, Italian, Spanish, and Greek, and grew to speak French as her first language. In other words, she became a Frenchwoman instead of a Scot.[lxxxv]

Mary's coming of age coincided with the tumultuous Scottish Reformation. A 1560 statistic reveals the extent to which the Scottish Catholic Church had succumbed to corruption of the financial kind: The Church's annual revenue that year was estimated to be £400,000 (ten times the Crown's revenue). Access to such ungodly wealth had attracted unspiritual nobles who were more interested in gaining tenure of church lands, using church property to their own ends, and collecting church revenues. As a result, Protestantism was increasingly gaining favor as a genuinely spiritual institution.

The European Reformation had been instigated by Martin Luther, a German Augustinian monk who insisted that the Scripture should be every Christian's guiding text. He rejected the pope's authority (an action that could lead to charges of heresy and death by burning at the stake at the time) and all Church practices that were not explicitly included within the Bible. With support from several German princes and the introduction of the printing press, Luther was able to spread his theories across Christian Europe, effectively creating bitter divisions between Catholics and Protestants in many nations, including Scotland.

Mary's Catholic affiliations set her against the prevailing religious trends of her time. Her father James V had merely flirted with Protestant ideas to incentivize the pope to grant him various tax concessions. When he died, however, Scotland's status as a staunchly Catholic nation was already in question. While traditionally Catholic, technological and social changes in Scotland had placed it increasingly at odds with Rome and its ancient doctrines. While Mary was blissfully unaware as a young child, both France and England waged a war to arrange for her hand in marriage. France was Catholic; England's Henry VIII had recently converted to Protestantism. During the "Rough Wooing," England launched several military invasions to force Mary's hand in marriage. The French retaliated by supporting the Scottish army with their own men and firepower. In the end, the French emerged as the victor.

Mary's mother thus brokered her first marriage, which sealed the diplomatic relationship between Scotland and France. She married Francis II, the eldest son of Henry and Catherine, in April 1558.[lxxxvi] As a child ruler, Mary's prospects were not entirely dim. Her noteworthy beauty—red-gold hair, amber-colored eyes, and statuesque height—and regal upbringing helped her embody the ideal of a Renaissance princess and earned a fair amount of admiration and support from the Scottish people. Her lack of political cunning, however, would eventually spell her downfall.

The Scottish Renaissance monarchy that James IV and James V had consolidated under the Stewart dynasty hung on a precipice. Protestant activism and anti-French sentiment brought about a revolt against Mary of Guise in 1559. Monasteries were plundered, and England's Queen Elizabeth I was prompted to send in English troops to suppress French ambitions on Scotland.[lxxxvii] After Mary of Guise's death in June the following year, France and England both agreed to withdraw their troops from Scotland via the Treaty of Edinburgh.

Mary would eventually return to Scotland as an eighteen-year-old widow after the premature death of her husband in 1560 (due to an ear infection). While she was still abroad, Scotland's official religion was reformed to Protestantism, and her return to the British Isles was certainly unwelcome. The Scottish nobility saw her as an undesirable Roman Catholic princess, while Elizabeth I saw her status as the next in line to the English throne (via her Tudor ancestry) as a threat. Elizabeth I herself had divisions between Catholics and Protestants to contend with on English soil. The English Roman Catholics considered her to be an illegitimate queen since her father Henry VIII had divorced Catherine of Aragon to marry her mother, Anne Boleyn. They conspired to dethrone Elizabeth I and replace her with Mary.

Despite this treacherous political landscape, Mary initially managed a successful reign as the Queen of Scotland. With the help of her half-brother James, Earl of Moray,[lxxxviii] she practiced a policy of religious tolerance and charmed the common people with her beauty and grace. She also brokered a semblance of peace with the difficult Scottish nobility, who were more interested in pursuing their own ends than demonstrating any real loyalty to the Crown. Mary's decision to follow her heart instead of her head catalyzed the events that led to her tragic downfall.

In July 1565, she decided to marry her handsome cousin Henry Stewart, Earl of Darnley.[lxxxix] This decision further alienated Elizabeth, who did not appreciate Mary marrying a Tudor descendant. Jealous of Darnley's ascent to power, her half-brother James rebelled and stopped supporting her. Darnley had little merit as a spouse or political ally. His capacity for petty cruelty is best demonstrated by his decision to murder Mary's Italian secretary and confidant David Rizzio right in front of her.[xc] (He alleged that Rizzio was having an affair with his wife). With the help of a group of Protestant nobles, he ambushed Mary as she dined with Rizzio and five close friends. Mary was heavily pregnant with Darnley's child at the time, but this did nothing to stop them from dragging Rizzio from the table. He was stabbed no less than 56 times in the adjacent room.

The arrival of Mary's son, James, did nothing to halt the deterioration of their marriage. Now in possession of an heir, Mary looked for a means to exit this untenable arrangement. Her actions would prove to be highly controversial, even if the full complicity in the death of her husband remains unknown. What is known is this: During the night of February 9, 1567, Darnley was recovering from a serious illness in a house on the outer parts of Edinburgh. This house was blown up, and Darnley was found strangled to death (he survived the blast and was attempting an escape when killed). A mere three months later, Mary married James Hepburn, the Earl of Bothwell, an adventurer and the chief suspect in Darnley's murder.[xci]

Mary's opponents alleged that she had been in an adulterous relationship with Hepburn, who had murdered Darnley to rise to power. Another theory is that Darnley had been plotting to murder Mary but was killed by his own trap. Whatever her intentions and affections for Hepburn were, it was a politically suicidal move. It reflected Mary's own deteriorating mental health and lack of a wise counselor to support her decision-making process in a treacherous time. The Scottish nobility revolted against their queen and her consort. They were permanently separated at Carberry Hill on June 15, 1567. Hepburn was exiled and imprisoned until his death in 1578.

Mary was sentenced to imprisonment in Lochleven Castle and forced to abdicate. Her one-year-old son James was crowned as King of Scotland in her place. Mary still had supporters though who helped her escape from prison in 1568. After they were defeated at Langside, she fled to England to seek refuge under the care of her cousin Elizabeth I. Instead, Elizabeth I deftly used Darnley's murder as an excuse to imprison Mary in England. As her half-brother James Moray excelled at being the regent of Scotland, Mary languished in several prisons over the following 18 years of her life.

Elizabeth I was pressured by her Protestant supporters to eliminate her Catholic rival to the throne, but she was not unsympathetic to her cousin's plight. She kept Mary under surveillance and left her to find some peace in religion, embroidery, and small pets. Mary pleaded unsuccessfully for her freedom and began turning to more risky means of securing it. She became the central figure of various Catholic plots that wanted to assassinate Elizabeth and replace her with Mary but was not directly involved in any of them. When she began corresponding with Anthony Babington who was scheming to depose Elizabeth though, her death sentence was sealed.

Francis Walsingham, Elizabeth's principal secretary and spymaster, intercepted those letters and used them as evidence to convince Elizabeth to place her cousin on trial. Her status as the sovereign queen of Scotland could not save her from being found guilty of treason. She was condemned to death in October 1586. Her cousin hesitated before signing her death warrant, but she eventually placed her name on the dotted line. As long as she lived, Mary would pose a danger to the English throne. She was executed at Fotheringhay Castle at the age of 44 on February 8, 1587. Years of physical inactivity had robbed her of her health and beauty, but she met her end with an unnerving grace. When her son, James VI of Scotland, succeeded Elizabeth I as the King of England in 1603, he exhumed her body from Peterborough Cathedral.[xcii] Her final resting place is a stately monument in the vault of King Henry VII's Chapel in Westminster Abbey. This was James' royal way of commemorating the mother he never knew—the woman who allowed him to become the King of Scotland *and* England.

Mary's legacy as a compelling ill-fated figure of Scottish and English history lives on. Her opponents denounced her as an adulteress and a conniving murderess, whereas others saw her as a tragic and romantic character deserving of sympathy. Modern cinema has certainly been sympathetic to her life story. She has been portrayed (as the main protagonist) by four-time Oscar-winning American actress Katharine Hepburn in 1936, English actress Vanessa Redgrave in 1971, bilingual French actress Camille Rutherford in 2013, and Irish and American Oscar-nominated actress Saoirse Ronan in 2018.

Chapter 10 – The King of Great Britain

Unlike his mother, James VI did not fall victim to the bitter divisions between the Scottish factions who were pro-Catholic and those who were Protestant-leaning. His early life was fairly isolated, but his solid education helped to prepare him not only for the Scottish kingship but also as a monarch on the European stage. When he was 12, he got his first taste of leading the government when the Earl of Morton was removed from the regency in 1578. In 1581, James VI took decisive control over his kingdom from the succession of regents who had been in power ever since he was born. He would soon prove that he was no longer content with serving as a puppet for the various factions vying for supremacy and power.

He soon realized that he had more to gain from an alliance with Elizabeth I as opposed to joining forces with all her opponents. In 1586, they became formal allies via the Treaty of Berwick. When Elizabeth signed Mary's death warrant the following year, James VI merely voiced meek and formal protests. With his mother dead and Elizabeth I facing old age without an heir, he was effectively next in line to the English throne.

By the time James VI married Anne,[xciii] the daughter of Frederick II of Denmark, he had established a firm centralized authority. With great political intelligence and a knack for diplomacy, he played off the Protestant and Roman Catholic nobles against each other to maintain his position. He also had the effective aid of the Octavians, a group of commissioners that helped him rival Elizabeth I in terms of the absoluteness of her rule. Despite being baptized as a Catholic at Stirling Castle as a young boy, James VI became a devout Presbyterian.[xciv] He arranged to appoint himself the head of Scotland's Presbyterian Church, a position which granted him the power to appoint its bishops.

In March 1603, the moment that James VI had been waiting for arrived. Elizabeth I died, allowing James VI of Scotland to become James I of England and Ireland. This transition of power was surprisingly smooth; James VI relocated to London and only returned to Scotland once after that in 1617. The first few years of his reign were a time of peace and prosperity for both kingdoms. After only one year on the throne, he ended England's costly war with Spain. He also tried to arrange a marriage between the Spanish Infanta (Philip III's eldest daughter Anne) and his son but was unsuccessful. His daughter Elizabeth was married to Frederick, the Elector of the Palatinate (a historical region in Germany) and a leader of the German Protestants.

James VI's early education instilled literary ambitions that were quite unusual in princes and kings. This can be partly attributed to the influence of his tutor George Buchanan, a noted historian and poet.[xcv] Over the years, James VI's body of political writings grew to include *The True Lawe of Free Monarchies* (1598) and *Basilikon Doron* (1599), as well as a collection of poems and political essays. His most famous and enduring literary contribution, however, was the newly authorized English translation of the Bible which was published in 1611. The King James Version of the Bible became the standard issue for over 250 years since it was first published.[xcvi] There was a need for the English Bible to be revised after the Reformation since many deemed the existing translations to be "corrupt and not answerable to the truth of the original." The King James Version was inevitably found to be lacking in one regard or the other depending on who was doing the judging (Catholics wanted the new translation of the Bible to be more supportive of their doctrines vis-à-vis Protestantism; Puritans wanted James VI to introduce some of the Scottish Church's more radical ideas), but it is widely acknowledged as one of early modern England's most important literary accomplishments.

James VI was not content to simply have England and Scotland be symbolically united under the same monarch. He styled himself "King of Great Britain" with the aim of erasing the bitter divisions between England and Scotland and with the grandiose objective of unifying them into one entity. Weeks after he arrived in London, he proclaimed his grand ambitions for uniting the two longtime rivals. The commission of English and Scottish Members of Parliaments (MPs), that was established to assess the viability of such an endeavor, ultimately found themselves being unable to agree on this venture. They did, however, agree that England should repeal all of the hostile laws that it had introduced against the Scots over the years. At this point in time, Great Britain remained more of a symbolic aspiration than an actuality. The Union Jack, which combined the crosses of St. George and St. Andrew, was nevertheless there to stay.

Naturally, there were blemishes on James VI's legacy. Apart from failing to convince Westminster of the viability of a total union between England and Scotland, he often antagonized them with his theories about a monarch's divine right to rule (i.e., royal absolutism).[xcvii] He also incurred their wrath by constantly demanding additional funds to pay for all of his extravagant expenditures (his spending habits were especially intolerable given the costs that had recently been incurred through England's long war with Spain). In the end, no compromise could be reached between the dictatorial king and an increasingly self-assertive Parliament that demanded the right to shape public policy. In 1611, James VI dissolved the Parliament after a series of conflicts. After the death of James VI's competent chief minister Robert Cecil in 1612, his judgment only deteriorated over the years.

Despite these shortcomings, England and Scotland were closer than ever before during James VI's reign. The earlier centuries of incessant conflict were replaced by increasing cultural and economic assimilation (the two kingdoms remained politically distinct, despite James VI's desire for a complete union). The English and Scottish Churches were also united in their shared interests in preserving the Reformation and fending off Roman Catholic plans to undermine it. A new dilemma arose in the Scottish national consciousness. Did they want to pursue a complete and totalizing union with England or revert back to a time when the two kingdoms were utterly separated?

Chapter 11 – The Union and The Scottish Enlightenment

James VI died in March 1625 and was succeeded by his son, Charles I, who had no interest in realizing his father's vision of a united Scotland and England.[xcviii] And yet, the Act of Union would be signed in less than a century after he assumed the throne.[xcix] On May 1, 1707, Scotland and England united under the name of Great Britain. For the first time in history, the Scottish Parliament would be disbanded; its MPs would represent Scottish interests through their seats in Westminster.

The road to this political milestone was anything but smooth sailing. Like his father, Charles I's insistence on his divine right to rule ran afoul of an increasingly critical and antagonistic Parliament. Having been raised in England all his life, his utter lack of affinity with Scotland and its people and institutions earned him the disfavor of the Scottish nobility. He alienated them further by pursuing wars with Spain and France, which advanced English interests but disrupted Scottish trade interests. By 1641, a revolutionary situation was at hand in both kingdoms after Charles I attempted to implement anti-Catholic changes in the English and Scottish Churches. After two bitter civil wars, Charles I's supporters were defeated. He was charged with high treason and "other high crimes against the realm of England." On January 30, 1649, he was sentenced to death.

Oliver Cromwell, an English soldier and statesman who had led Parliament against Charles I, then assumed his role as the Lord Protector of England, Scotland, and Ireland.[c] He declared England to be a commonwealth and a free state. Determined to restore England to the status it enjoyed under Elizabeth I, he introduced an incorporated parliamentary union in Scotland. Despite the general lack of support, his administrative efficiency and impartial judiciary effectively maintained order and peace across both kingdoms. Any possibility of dissent was stifled by Cromwell's readiness to use sheer force.

The monarchy was eventually restored on May 14, 1660, when Charles II was proclaimed King of Great Britain and Ireland. When he was succeeded by his brother James VII, however, James VII's deep desire to establish an absolutist rule in both kingdoms and to reinstate a Catholic monarchy instigated widespread turmoil.[ci] His Protestant opponents invited Prince William III of Orange, husband of James' Protestant daughter Mary, to lead the charge against their intolerably pro-Catholic king.[cii] William's show of force was successful, forcing James VII to escape to France. Prince William III of Orange was offered the English crown in April 1689 and the Scottish crown the following month. The 1689 Bill of Rights, nevertheless, stipulated that monarchs could no longer govern without the consent of their parliaments.

These prolonged periods of internal conflict had severely weakened the Scottish economy. When the idea of a union between England and Scotland resurfaced as William III of Orange was offered the English crown, the Scottish elite were in favor of the proposal. The union would also help to enshrine Protestantism in both kingdoms and stave off attacks from ex-King James and his pro-Catholic supporters. There was, nevertheless, still a significant amount of anti-English sentiment among the Scottish masses. It would take far more extenuating circumstances—William III's unexpected death from a horse-riding fall, a new war between Britain and France, a Scottish Parliament revolt, and additional accommodations for Scotland in terms of trade, religion, and taxes—for Scotland to finally warm up to the idea of a union. They were partly persuaded by an attractive carrot (access to a unified free trade area) and two dire sticks (England would ban all imports of Scottish staple products if Scotland refused the terms for a union, and Scots would lose their rights to English property).[ciii]

The benefits of a union to Scotland, with its guarantee of free trade and safeguards for Scotland's national church and legal system, can be seen in the Scottish Enlightenment.[civ] One may not simply conclude a clear cause and effect scenario here, but it is evident that the newfound era of peace and prosperity under this arrangement allowed for the unprecedented evolution of Scottish intellectual life. Scottish intellectual accomplishments from the 1750s onward earned Edinburgh descriptors such as a "hotbed of genius."

From the sciences to philosophy to economics, Scottish thinkers became international leaders in their field. The Scottish Enlightenment's hall of fame includes historian and philosopher David Hume,[cv] philosopher Adam Smith,[cvi] historian William Robertson, poet Robert Burns, architect Robert Adam and his brother James, mathematician Colin Maclaurin, physiologist William Cullen, chemist Joseph Black, geologist James Hutton,[cvii] and engineers James Watt and Thomas Telford. Their wide-ranging intellectual accomplishments were evidence of a robust Scottish educational system, which advocated for intellectual curiosity and the practical applications of knowledge.

James Hutton, David Hume, and Adam Smith would eventually be recognized as three of the most influential intellectuals in the history of Europe. Hutton's contributions as a geologist were crucial in ushering in an age of religious skepticism. Hutton introduced the then-groundbreaking concept of uniformitarianism, which explains the various features of the Earth's crust by means of natural processes over time such as erosion, sedimentation, deposition, and upthrusting. By using precise calculations to determine the age of rocks in Scotland, Hutton had scientific evidence that the Earth was much, much older than the 6,000 years the Bible had claimed. Hutton's findings contributed to his conviction that it was scientific discoveries and not religion that should be used to understand the laws of the natural world. His 1785 publication, *A Theory of the Earth*, became the founding text for modern geology.

On the other hand, David Hume made immense contributions to the field of philosophy. An intellectual of many stripes—philosopher, historian, economist, essayist—he was known for his skepticism and philosophical empiricism. At only 28, he returned to Scotland from France with the publication of his groundbreaking work, *A Treatise on Human Nature*. Like Hutton, Hume was invested in a secular and scientific worldview that moved firmly away from the Christian theological worldview that had shaped much of Scotland's past. He drew from the works of English physicist Sir Isaac Newton and English philosopher John Locke. Hume intended to explain humanity without referring to God or religion and turned to scientific reasoning to do so. For him, morality was not a product of God's creation. Instead, it was a product of human reason and sentiment—a practical imperative that motivates us to differentiate between right and wrong. Hume understood that people were not purely rational beings; emotions, sentiments, and passions played a significant role in shaping one's thoughts and rationality. Hume was also a brave and outspoken critic of religion, and he boldly questioned the veracity of miracles. On his deathbed, Hume was cheerfully unperturbed by the possibility of a Christian afterlife where he would be judged harshly for his atheism.

Finally, Adam Smith was a moral philosopher that is credited as the father of modern economics. *An Inquiry into the Nature and Causes of the Wealth of Nations* is a seminal text that is still widely read in economics courses across the world. Smith was strongly motivated to understand how money was circulated and its impact on society. Smith's scholarship was crucial in understanding how the rapidly evolving commercial economy that emerged throughout the Industrial Revolution had bearings on everyday life and national policy. Smith was invested in economic efficiency and free trade, but he was not oblivious to the detrimental effects that the pursuit of wealth could engender. He deemed economic progress to be synonymous with societal progress. The purely profit-driven interests of Glasgow's Tobacco Lords and the existence of slavery were deemed to be undesirable rungs on the ladder toward a more enlightened civilization. Smith's economic ideas were also crucial to Britain's decision to end the American War of Independence. Smith's position as an eminent economic thinker allowed him to influence the British prime minister so that Britain would gain more wealth by trading with America instead of attempting to ensure that it remained a subservient colony.

Chapter 12 – The Industrial Revolution

In the early 1700s, Scotland was mostly a rural and agricultural economy. It only had a population of one million people, with a relatively small portion based in its modest urban townships. Within the course of a single lifetime, everything changed. By the 1820s, the effects of the Industrial Revolution were unmistakable.[cviii] The scientific theories that had been conceptualized during the Scottish Enlightenment swiftly turned into practical applications that could be turned into hearty profits in a capitalist world.

Scotland's population rose dramatically. People left the countryside and traditional farm life for manufacturing towns, which eventually became bustling cities. There were approximately 1.5 million people in Scotland during the start of the 19th century. By the end of the 20th century, this number had tripled to over 4.5 million people. A significant portion of this rise can be attributed to immigrants, particularly Irish immigrants who were fleeing the prospect of starvation during the Irish Potato Famine (1845–1849).[cix]

This population rise was also partly the byproduct of crucial advancements in medicine, healthcare, and public health standards. These improvements reduced the mortality rate in the face of previously fatal epidemic diseases. Meanwhile, the scientific innovations that were assimilated into traditional agricultural practices allowed fewer farmers to produce enough produce to feed a larger population. Southeastern farmers were praised for their efficiency, northeastern farmers for their cattle and beef, and Ayrshire (a county in the southwest) for the large quantities of quality milk their cows produced.[cx]

Innovations in chemistry (e.g., the use of chlorine to bleach linen) helped make the Scottish textile industry surpass agriculture. Linen production became more efficient than ever before with the use of newly discovered chemicals and the adoption of English inventions like Hargreaves' spinning jenny, Arkwright's water frame, and Crompton's mule. These inventions transformed the weaving process, radically increasing output, productivity, and competitiveness. Instead of relying on manpower alone, these new spinning machines were powered by massive water wheels. The old tradition of men working on handlooms was replaced by an efficient factory system. Women and children were roped into the workforce, spending long hours toiling for relatively low wages.

During the 1830s, heavy industry replaced textiles as the most important component of the Scottish economy. The production of coal and iron rose tremendously, facilitating the popularization of railways, steam locomotives, and ships. The use of canals and horses as the dominant forms of transportation slowly became obsolete. If the first phase of the Industrial Revolution consisted of old industries becoming more efficient through the adoption of new technologies, the second phase was driven by Scottish innovations themselves. Henry Bell (1767–1830) built the *Comet*, the first successful passenger steamship, in 1812. It catalyzed the birth of the Scottish shipbuilding industry and the railway industry. James Watt (1736–1819) did not invent the steam engine as commonly believed (it had existed since the early 18th century), but he did invent the separate condenser (which reduced the amount of water steam engines needed while allowing them to produce more power).

The introduction of an extensive railway network helped Scotland to make significant economic progress during the Victorian era. When Queen Victoria assumed the throne in 1827, there were only a few Scottish railway lines in existence. These were mainly used to transport coal and other industrial raw materials between the bustling urban hubs of Glasgow, Edinburgh, and Dundee. In 1843, the Edinburgh-Glasgow railway line opened, catalyzing a national obsession with railways. Within a single generation, practically all of Scotland's railways were built, constituting some of the world's most ambitious engineering projects at the time. Railway tracks were built between small villages and major towns, stretching in all directions. Thanks to the advent of efficient steam engines, journeys that would have taken days on horse-drawn carriages were now completed in a matter of hours.

There was, of course, a dark side to all of this intellectual, economic, and technological progress. The extensive railway network may have effectively bridged the distance between the urban centers and the countryside, allowing tourism in rural Scotland to boom, but urban growth during the Victorian era had created dirty, overcrowded, and polluted cities, with Glasgow being the primary example. The lack of adequate housing for the huge influx of migrants led to the sprawl of slums with dire standards of living. With over 20,000 people forced to live in shabby housing and practically no sanitation, one can only imagine the effect of such conditions on the body and mind.

> In the very centre of the city there was an accumulated mass of squalid wretchedness unequalled in any other town in the British Dominions. There was concentrated everything wretched, dissolute, loathsome and pestilential. Dunghills lie in the vicinity of dwellings, and from the extremely defective sewerage filth of every kind constantly accumulates.[cxi]

These dismal living conditions were incredibly conducive to disease. Glasgow soon became a hotbed for typhus and typhoid. Scotland's participation in the global British Empire also led to a deadly outbreak of cholera. In 1832, the first cholera outbreak in Scotland killed 3,000 people in Glasgow alone. All the public health advances that had been achieved since the Black Death were temporarily reversed as death rates soared. It appears obvious now, but the link between dirt and disease was not immediately apparent then. It was only after the subsequent cholera epidemics of 1848 and 1853 that the medical community identified the filthy living conditions as a problem that had to be solved. The introduction of an expensive sewage system and a clean water supply from Loch Katrine was crucial in improving sanitation and public health standards in Glasgow.

Eager to escape the grimness of city life, many wealthier Scots took the opportunity to breathe in the fresh air and enjoy the stunning vistas of the Scottish countryside.[cxii] They also developed appetites for hunting deer, shooting birds, and fishing. By the 1890s, there were widespread concerns that urban-rural tourism was devastating the countryside and causing various species of bird and deer to lean toward extinction.

Apart from the rising pollution levels and the desecration of nature for the extraction of raw materials, Scotland's relentless appetite for wealth and progress incurred heavy ethical costs. As Scotland looked beyond its traditional trading relationships with France and the Low Countries (Netherlands, Belgium, and western Germany), it became complicit in the imperial exploitation of countries and populations outside of Europe. The Scottish textile industry developed a dependence on imported cotton from India, England's prized colonial possession, as well as the slave plantations of America.

Scottish capitalists also proved to be adept at extracting profits from the Atlantic tobacco trade. There were no tobacco plantations in Scotland, but Glasgow's infamous Tobacco Lords were able to gain a firm grip on the trade through their strategic position (Glasgow was closer to the transatlantic shipping routes than London or Bristol) and savvy use of capital. Their agents sailed out to North Carolina and Virginia to trade with the owners of small tobacco plantations. They provided credit and loaned them tools, wrought from Scottish iron, and Scottish-made linen, which would later be repaid with takings from their future crops. As these plantations grew in size and scale with the help of their funding, so did the amount of tobacco that made its way to Glasgow's warehouses.

Tobacco was only one component of Scotland's Three Way Trade with the rapidly evolving American economy.[cxiii] Ships from Scotland would also sail to Africa to be filled with slaves. These slaves would then be taken to either tobacco plantations in America or sugar plantations in the West Indies. The ships would return to Scottish ports with the products of this exploitative labor system (primarily sugar and tobacco). This arrangement also brought in large amounts of profits into Scotland, which could then be reinvested into the Scottish Industrial Revolution. In 1747, the Tobacco Lords became even wealthier when the French government gave Glasgow a lucrative monopoly over the supply of tobacco to France. The huge influx of money into Scotland's rising number of banks facilitated the growth of a financial industry and newfangled forms of credit.

Chapter 13 – Decline

After the triumphs of the Scottish Enlightenment and the Industrial Revolution, Scotland found itself in an arc of decline. World War I (July 8, 1914–November 11, 1918) coincided not only with the loss of many Scottish lives (over 140,000 Scottish soldiers were killed) but also with widespread economic decline.[cxiv] Trouble was brewing even before the war. The Singer Sewing Factory strike in 1911 was a clear indication of the untenable working conditions in the majority of Scotland's factories. In 1915, the lack of housing, high rental fees, and the poor quality of existing housing led to mass rent strikes in Glasgow.

Given these generally dismal conditions, it is not surprising that many Scottish men volunteered to fight against Germany during World War I. While their Victorian English counterparts thought little about the prospect of being a soldier, their Scottish counterparts' psyche had been indelibly shaped by years of tribal infighting and conflict with the English military. In 1914, Scotland made up less than 10 percent of Great Britain's pre-World War population. However, Scotsmen comprised 13 percent of the volunteers that enlisted in the British Army between 1914 and 1915. To distinguish themselves from their English comrades, they fought in plaid kilts, wore sporrans (a traditional Scottish pouch that functioned as a pocket on the pocket-free kilt), and marched to military tunes emitted by bagpipes. On the home front, Scotland suffered from its first ever air raid. On April 2, 1916, two German Zeppelins dropped bombs over the fields of Northumberland and the city of Edinburgh. Between 100,000 and 148,000 Scottish men and women died during World War I.

Marriage and birth rates increased after World War I ended in 1918, leading to Scotland's own baby boom in 1920. That year, 137,000 babies were born—a dramatic statistic that was not matched by the baby boom Scotland experienced after World War II. By 1919, Scotland's population was estimated to reach 4.8 million people— the highest number of people since 1855. Scotland's population would eventually peak at nearly 4.9 million in 1922 when the postwar optimism waned in the face of economic hardship.

The socialist movement and trade union activism only intensified as it became evident that the incredible expansion of heavy industry in the 1920s was actually an overexpansion. The war had created a short-lived demand for production from Scotland's coal mining, shipbuilding, and engineering industries. After it ended, the fall in demand for new ships decimated Scottish shipbuilding by a staggering 90% of its initial size. Meanwhile, increasing foreign competition put over 50% of Scotland's iron furnaces out of business by 1927. The Scottish industries also suffered as Germany, Eastern Europe, and Russia ceased to be export markets for Scottish goods due to political factors. The introduction of new technologies and production methods also played a role in reducing the number of jobs that required manual labor.

The economic depression that plagued Britain throughout the 1920s and 30s was particularly acute in Scotland. Scotland was home to the poorest living conditions in all of Great Britain along with high rates of unemployment. With the economy in ruins after four years of warfare, thousands of Scots decided to leave the British Isles for the chance of a better life in the colonies. Between 1841 to 1931, over two million Scots emigrated abroad—the highest emigration rate for any European country during this period. Unskilled laborers sought better fortunes on the shores of Canada and Australia, while their skilled counterparts sought to recreate their middle-class lives in South Africa and the United States. This "brain drain" cost Scotland many of its skilled and educated men and women. Meanwhile, approximately 749,000 Scots relocated to other parts of Great Britain (primarily England).

It is not surprising that these trying economic conditions were a breeding ground for political radicalism. When the General Strike unfolded in 1926 (where all union workers across the nation refused to work unless they were granted better pay and improved working conditions), tanks and soldiers lined the streets in anticipation of a Communist revolution. The Liberal Party found their influence waning, while the Unionist Party, Labour Party, and the Scottish National Party (SNP) gained widespread support and popularity.

Scottish resilience was tested once again during World War II (September 1, 1939–September 2, 1945) when Scotland became a target for aggressive German bombing raids.[cxv] This time, Scottish civilians would not be spared the suffering that their sailors, pilots, and soldiers endured as they fought against Adolf Hitler's formidable army. Nazi pilots took aim at Scotland's hubs to target its crucial heavy industry factories. During the nights of March 13 and 14, 1941, the industrial hub of Clydebank in Glasgow suffered from sustained bombing.

The death count on the home front was reduced by the preemptive evacuation of children and their mothers in the cities to the countryside, but this also caused a major disruption to everyday life.[cxvi] Many families had to be separated during the evacuation process, causing significant psychological trauma to the younger children. They also had to make do with strict food rationing during the war, which limited their daily food intake to small portions of tea, jam, butter, sugar, and cheese.

After the first wave of bombing raids, the Scots lived in fear of subsequent attacks. They were thankfully spared the agony and devastation when Hitler decided to focus German military efforts on an ill-advised attack on Russia. When the Axis parties finally surrendered, Scotland had lost approximately 34,000 soldiers and 6,000 civilians. Efforts were made to reduce unemployment and restore the health of the Scottish economy but to mixed results. Agricultural productivity was sustained, but Scotland's heavy industries (e.g., shipbuilding and coal mining) would never recover.

Chapter 14: Scottish Feminism

Scotland's involvement in the two World Wars had major and longstanding ramifications on gender roles in Scottish society. Before the war, Scottish women had been pressured to conform to the Victorian ideal of being the "angel in the home." Women from the middle and working classes were very much expected to faithfully perform the duties of a wife and mother. The opportunity to attend university or to pursue a career alongside their male counterparts was typically out of the equation. The men were expected to bring home the proverbial bacon, while the women were expected to take care of the home and children.[cxvii]

This did not mean that women were completely absent from the workforce prior to the wars. Young unmarried women, spinsters, and widows who did not have a man to rely on often pursued careers in stereotypically "feminine" professions: nursing, childcare, and teaching. They were paid less than their male counterparts and were not considered to be of equal standing, but these forms of employment, nevertheless, allowed them to take up roles and positions beyond the confines of domesticity.

Working class women, who often had larger families than their middle-class counterparts, were usually forced to work due to economic necessity. To supplement their husband's income, they often worked on a part-time basis as a cook, cleaner, or nanny for wealthier families. The labor they performed—in addition to the challenging duties of caring for their own children—was rarely considered as "real work," which was then perceived to be an exclusively male domain. When a 1911 census revealed that only 1 in 20 working Scottish women were married, it probably excluded all the part-time work performed by working-class women.

The First World War radically altered this status quo. As large numbers of able-bodied Scottish men enlisted in the military, they left behind sizable numbers of vacancies in the factories. Scottish women thus seized the opportunity to perform in the work roles they had previously been excluded from. They also gained a political voice by joining trade unions. When the men who survived the war returned home and resumed their factory work, they found that their female counterparts were in a significantly stronger bargaining position.[cxviii]

The opportunity to participate in the workforce had been particularly advantageous for working-class women, who had been largely overlooked by the pre-war suffragette movement. Before WWI, the Women's Social and Political Union (WSPU) had largely advocated for voting rights to be extended to middle-class, property-owning women. This exclusive and narrow advocacy was democratized when large numbers of working-class women gained a platform for their concerns via trade union membership. In 1918, women over 30 could vote regardless of class. In 1928, women finally gained equal voting rights.[cxix]

Societal changes in attitudes toward sex, contraception, marriage, and motherhood during the early 20th century also played a significant part in the lives of Scottish women. The very same year that women over 30 gained the opportunity to vote, Edinburgh-born Marie Stopes published an important treatise of marriage and feminism titled *Married Love*.[cxx] Stopes decried the traditional gendered division of labor which prevented women from fully participating in public life. She advocated for a more equal division of household labor and childcare duties that would allow women to pursue their own careers and lives beyond the domestic sphere. She was also a pioneer in her advocacy for birth control, which granted women more control over their bodies and life choices. Contraception may often be taken for granted today, but this was a highly controversial topic during Stopes' lifetime. Stopes went against the pope and church leaders, but she did have the backing of the medical community. Stopes was not content with just being a bestselling author and public figure. She went on to form the Mother's Clinic for Constructive Birth Control in Holloway, London, in 1921. She also influenced the formation of the National Birth Control Association in 1931, which paved the way for the introduction of the Family Planning Act in 1967. Stopes' influence is evident in the consistent decline in Scottish birth rates, which halved between the late 1870s and early 1930s.

The Second World War allowed Scottish women to participate more actively in the labor market once again. As their male counterparts took to the skies, seas, and battlefields, women staffed the Women's Land Army and vacant factories. While they were barred from battling on the front lines, they did support the British military through their participation in the Women's Voluntary Service (WVS), Auxiliary Territorial Service (ATS), and the Women's Auxiliary Air Force (WAAF). The changing attitudes toward women's capabilities and the urgency of the war allowed Scottish women to take on highly technical engineering jobs. For example, over 10,000 women were employed at the Rolls-Royce factory at Hillington (near Glasgow) where they built the Merlin engines that were essential to Spitfires and Lancaster Bombers.

Despite this progress, Scottish women still struggled to gain equal pay. A larger proportion of women managed to remain in the workforce after World War II ended compared to World War I. This was partly due to the recovering economy and the creation of the welfare state. The availability of state benefits was particularly beneficial to the working classes. With more career opportunities and government aid for their children and elderly dependents, women were able to make great strides in improving their overall standard of living. By the 1960s, most Scottish women who worked were married—there was effectively no longer a stigma against working mothers and wives. The decline of the heavy industries in the 1970s led to more job opportunities in clerical work, secretarial work, the service sector, and light manufacturing—precisely the kind of jobs that were less inclined to discriminate against women. Full parity remains a distant reality, but there is no denying the great strides that Scottish women have achieved in education, the labor force, and political representation.

While Mary, Queen of Scots, had once been perceived as an unfit ruler due to her gender, Nicola Sturgeon made history as the first female First Minister of Scotland in 2014 (i.e., the leader of the Scottish government).[cxxi] Born in 1970, Sturgeon cited British Prime

Minister Margaret Thatcher as her inspiration for participating in politics at a young age. At only 16, Sturgeon decided to join the Scottish National Party. Thatcher, who was known around the world as the "Iron Lady," was a positive role model because she demonstrated that a woman could reach the uppermost ranks of political power. As a policymaker, however, Sturgeon found little common ground with her. As a teenager, Sturgeon was deeply opposed to Thatcher's conservative policies, which were highly unpopular in Scotland.

Sturgeon went on to pursue a law degree at the University of Glasgow and became a solicitor for a Glasgow law firm. Her ambitions, nevertheless, remained within the field of politics. During Britain's 1992 general election, Sturgeon became Scotland's youngest parliamentary candidate (she was nearly 22). She did not win a seat, but her place at the table was earned in 1999. As a member of the Scottish Parliament, she took on a prominent role in the National Executive Committee, and she worked in the domains of health, education, and justice.

In June 2004, Sturgeon made her ambitions for the leadership of the SNP known when John Swinney resigned. She eventually withdrew her candidacy in favor of Alex Salmond, who had been the party leader before Swinney replaced him in 2000. Sturgeon became Salmond's running mate and was rewarded with the deputy leader position when he won the election. Since Salmond was an MP at Westminster and not a member of the Scottish Parliament in Edinburgh, however, Sturgeon was the de facto leader of the SNP contingent in Edinburgh. She gained a solid reputation for her leadership and oratory prowess. Under her leadership, the SNP emerged as the largest party in the Scottish Parliament after the 2007 elections. Salmon became Scotland's first minister, while Sturgeon became the Deputy First Minister of Scotland and Minister for Public Health and Wellbeing. In 2014, Salmond resigned as the First Minister of Scotland and leader of the SNP, allowing Sturgeon to take her place as Scotland's first female head of state since Mary, Queen   of   Scots.

Chapter 15: LGBTI Rights in Scotland

As with women's rights, Scotland has made significant progress in the field of LGBTI rights in recent decades. For much of its history, religious attitudes led to widespread discrimination against gay, lesbian, bisexual, and transgender individuals in Scotland. Scottish attitudes toward the question of homosexuality did not significantly depart from the United Kingdom until after World War II.[cxxii]

In post-World War II Britain, there was a significant increase in the prosecution of gay men for homosexual crimes in England and Wales. Policemen would often use a strategy of entrapment—posing as gay men looking for sexual encounters in popular "cruising" spots—to arrest men who were actively seeking sexual liaisons. Some of the most high-profile arrests in British history include the English author Oscar Wilde in 1895, English computer scientist Alan Turing in 1952, and the Wildeblood scandal in 1954. The increasing frequency of arrests prompted the government to form the Wolfenden Committee in 1954. Led by Sir John Wolfenden, it consulted legal representatives, religious leaders, legislators, and civic leaders to address the issue of homosexual behavior.

In 1957, the Departmental Committee on Homosexual Offences and Prostitution in Great Britain submitted its report.[cxxiii] This marked the first time that a British government participated in public discourse on homosexuality and the rights of sexual minorities in the nation. While the report did not condone or sanction homosexual behavior or same-sex relationships, it did argue that the criminalization of homosexuality was an injustice to civil liberty. It argued that one's sexual orientation and preferences were a private matter of morality. It also advocated for medical treatment to "correct" homosexual desires and behaviors and for children and adults to be protected from homosexual activity. The medical treatments that arrested gay men would often be subjected to would be deemed highly unethical by modern standards. They usually involved electroconvulsive therapy (ECT) and estrogen therapy.

A decade later, the recommendations made by the Wolfenden Report contributed to the 1967 Sexual Offences Act. Its primary contribution to LGBTI rights was the decriminalization of homosexuality in England and Wales. However, Scotland and Northern Ireland were exempted from these reforms. The resistance toward the Wolfenden recommendations was particularly strong in Scotland. Dr. Gayle Davis, a social historian working at the University of Edinburgh, noted that the general consensus was that Scotland was not ready to accept LGBTI individuals:

> There's a lot of resistance to Wolfenden in Scotland, there's really a great deal. Law in fact can be quite resistant - lawyers themselves. And one of the reasons, kind of ironically, is because they argue Scotland has, basically, a more lenient legal system anyway. It's actually much more difficult to be prosecuted for homosexuality in Scotland than it is in England and Wales and therefore let's not touch it. We don't need to interfere.[cxxiv]

Scottish attitudes toward homosexuality became more progressive in the 1970s and 1980s, as the sexual revolution that was sparked in the United States coincided with a general decline in religious beliefs. Scotland finally decriminalized homosexuality in 1980 after activist groups, like the Scottish Minorities Group, brought their case to the European Court of Human Rights. When the Criminal Justice (Scotland) Act was introduced, Scotland was finally on par with England and Wales in terms of LGBTI rights.

Since then, Scotland has remarkably established a reputation as one of Europe's most progressive countries in the domain of LGBTI equality. The Scottish government has viewed its previous legal position on homosexuality as discrimination and made efforts to remove criminal records for gay men who were once persecuted by the justice system for their sexual orientation.[cxxv] The 2007 Adoption and Children (Scotland) Act 2007 gave same-sex couples the opportunity to adopt children together. Another milestone was achieved with the Sexual Offences (Scotland) Act of 2009, which removed sexual orientation and gender identity from the list of legal sexual offenses.

In 2010, the Equality Act was introduced to protect LGBTI individuals from hate crimes and discrimination on the basis of their sexual orientation. It also provided legal protection for transgender individuals at all stages of the gender reassignment process. In 2014, Scotland became the first country within the United Kingdom to legalize same-sex marriage via the Marriage and Civil Partnership (Scotland) Act 2014, which was passed by an overwhelming majority in the Scottish Parliament. It also began including intersex individuals within its equality framework that year, and it became one of the most inclusive LGBTI legislations in the world. The Scottish government has also announced its partnership with the Scottish Transgender Alliance (STA), with the aim of improving public understanding of the nuances and complexities of gender identity and reassignment surgeries. It has supported LGBTI activist organizations and made efforts to alleviate the bullying of LGBTI students and youths.

Given these milestones, it is not entirely surprising that Scotland was ranked the most inclusive European nation for LGBTI equality and human rights legislation in 2015 by the European Region of the International Lesbian, Gay, Bisexual, Trans, and Intersex Association (ILGA Europe).[cxxvi] Scotland met 92% of ILGA's 48-point criteria, beating other notably progressive European nations such as Belgium, Malta, and Sweden. Scotland's progressive attitudes are also evident in the fact that many of its politicians are openly gay, lesbian, or bisexual. This includes Kezia Dugdale (a former leader of the Scottish Labour Party), Ruth Davidson (Leader of the Scottish Conservative Party), Patrick Harvie (co-convener of the Scottish Green Party), and David Coburn (leader of the Scottish UK Independence Party).[cxxvii]

There have naturally been setbacks to the increasing representation of LGBTI identities in Scottish public life. In 2000, Scotland was embroiled in a bitter debate over a legal clause that banned the positive portrayal of same-sex relationships in school. While this legal clause was eventually overturned by the Scottish Parliament, it led to a widespread moral panic that Scottish children would fall victim to "gay propaganda" and "gay sex lessons" in schools. The influential "Keep the Clause" campaign was a bitter reminder of the persistence of a double standard for heterosexual and homosexual relationships.

In 2017, Scotland lost its top spot on the ILGA-Europe rankings, coming in second to Malta.[cxxviii] The United Kingdom, as a whole, came in third, losing out slightly to Norway. The Scottish National Party (SNP) attributed this setback to the Conservatives, who were deemed to have fallen behind in making reforms required by the equality law. Angela Crawley, the SNP candidate for Lanark and Hamilton East, noted that same-sex couples were still not granted equal pension rights and that not all LGBTI individuals were fully protected from discrimination. Further progress could also be made in providing more protection to trans and intersex individuals, as well as in providing asylum to individuals fleeing persecution for their sexual identities. As of April 2019, conversion therapy on minors has not been banned in Scotland.

Chapter 16: The Loch Ness Monster

Despite the contributions of many Scottish intellectuals to science and modernity, the perception of Scotland as a terrain steeped in folklore, legends, myths, and superstitions persists. The unique phenomenon of Nessie, a.k.a., the Loch Ness monster, is emblematic of the longstanding Scottish appetite for legends and folklore.

The Loch Ness monster became an international sensation when the image known as the "surgeon's photograph" was widely circulated in 1934.[cxxix] Photographic "evidence" was new, but stories and reports of the lake being home to a monster are ancient. Loch Ness comes in second to Loch Lomond in terms of surface area, but it comes in first when it comes to volume (it contains more freshwater than all the lakes in Wales and England combined). It also comes in second to Loch Morar in terms of depth. Given these unfathomable depths, there have long been speculations as to what mysterious lifeforms might thrive in its impenetrable waters.

The Picts left behind stone carvings that represent an unusual beast with flippers. A biography of St. Columba dating back to 565 CE is the first written account of a monster in the waters. It describes an incident where a monster bit a swimmer and then set its aggressive sights on another man. Columba made an effective intervention, ordering the monster to "go back" to the depths it came from. There have been various other sightings of a creature in the lake throughout the centuries since then.

These folktales took on a new life in the 1930s when a new road adjacent to Loch Ness allowed drivers a majestic view of the lake. In April 1933, a couple reported that they saw a large animal—akin to a "dragon or prehistoric monster"—crossing the road in front of their car and disappearing into the lake. A Scottish newspaper (the *Inverness Courier*) sensationalized the incident, which then sparked other sightings. The *Daily Mail* fueled the fires of speculation by commissioning a hunter named Marmaduke Wetherell to find the mysterious monster. He uncovered large footprints along the lake's shores, which he argued was indicative of the presence of a large animal that was six meters long. Zoologists from the Natural History Museum eventually pointed out that the tracks were bogus. They were all identical impressions made with a hippopotamus leg. It is unclear if Wetherell had made the tracks himself, or if he had simply stumbled upon someone else's hoax.

The *Daily Mail* went on to print the now-iconic photograph of the Loch Ness Monster in 1934. Taken by Robert Kenneth Wilson, an English physician, it appeared to show the monster's small head and long neck from a distance. The photograph created an international interest in Nessie. Many believed that it was a plesiosaur: a long-necked marine reptile that lived during the time of the dinosaurs. The theory was that a lone plesiosaur—or a few of them—had survived the widespread extinction that marked the end of the Cretaceous phase approximately 66 million years ago.

Popular culture has held fast to the idea of Nessie being a plesiosaur—a myth that is certainly more compelling than other interpretations of it being a long-necked newt, a large invertebrate, a misidentified tree trunk, a mirage, a Greenland shark, or a large eel. Scientists have discredited the idea by pointing out that plesiosaurs were probably cold-blooded reptiles that could only thrive in warm tropical waters and not in the cold depths of Loch Ness.[cxxx] They have also argued that the lake does not contain enough food to support a carnivorous reptile the size of a plesiosaur. And there is also the geological fact that the loch is only 10,000 years old. Before the last ice age, it had been a frozen block of ice for nearly 20,000 years.

Yet, the myth of Nessie persists despite the lack of scientific evidence. Nessie can be found in many poems, short stories, novels, movies, and documentaries. After many monster hunters failed to find any conclusive evidence of Nessie's existence, more organized efforts were initiated. The most famous effort to find Nessie would be Operation Deepscan in 1987. This sonar exploration cost a staggering £1 million. It involved a week-long trawling of the entire length of Loch Ness by a flotilla of 24 sonar-equipped boats. No large prehistoric creature was identified from this comprehensive search. Meanwhile, other photographs that seemingly depicted Nessie were proven to be hoaxes. In 1994, Wilson's enduring photograph was discredited as a plastic- and- wooden head appended to a toy submarine. The culprit was none other than Marmaduke Wetherell himself.

The Scottish Natural Heritage (SNH) even has a "partly serious, partly fun" code for what to do if Nessie is found.[cxxxi] Nessie would be treated as a protected new species and would not be harmed. After a DNA sample is obtained, it would be released back into Loch Ness. The local businesses and communities living near Loch Ness would also have to be consulted to prepare for the inevitable arrival of tourists from all over the world. As it is, the mere myth of Nessie is enough to compel the arrival of 400,000 visitors to Loch Ness each year—which only leads to a measly ten reports of a mysterious lake-dweller each year. One can only imagine the pandemonium that might ensue if a rare species was proven to exist there.

Even if Nessie is never found, it lives on in the Scottish popular imagination. It certainly is not the only fictional animal that lives on in the Scottish psyche.[cxxxii] There is a country, after all, that led to the unicorn being featured on the United Kingdom's national crest. There are also kelpies, which are water spirits that resemble horses and who are often disguised as humans in Scottish folklore. The Highlanders also have various superstitions that involve fairies, which are believed to inhabit the Isle of Skye. The collective stories and myths surrounding these creatures undoubtedly contribute to Scotland's tourism industry as it enchants visitors from far and wide to seek a glimpse—or merely gain a sense—of Scottish magic. Nessie alone is estimated to have contributed nearly $80 million to Scotland's economy each year in the early 21st century.

Chapter 17: Postwar Scotland

The end of World War II gave way to a new world order, one where the sun had clearly set on the once all-powerful British Empire. As former British colonies across the world began demanding and securing their independence, the very idea of "Britishness" was called into question. Like their English counterparts, Scotland turned inward to examine its own place in the world as efforts to rebuild the country were underway. The socialist government in the United Kingdom ushered in an age of austerity while the welfare state began ingraining itself as a defining feature of British life.

In 1961, the Scottish Council for Development and Industry confessed that "if there is a panacea for Scotland's economic problems we have not found it."[cxxxiii] The economy may have improved after the end of World War II, but the decline in Scottish heavy industries still led to an unemployment rate that was twice as high as Britain's. The emerging light engineering and consumer goods industries did not create enough jobs to offset the jobs lost by the rapid disappearance of Scotland's coal-mining, steel, and shipbuilding industries. While many saw the importance of diversifying the economy, the managers of small Scottish firms and the government were relatively inefficient at taking the necessary steps to achieve this.

Margaret Thatcher's inauguration as prime minister in 1979 and the policies of deregulation and privatization that followed inspired widespread sentiments that Scottish interests were being unfairly discriminated against.[cxxxiv] Thatcher's stoic insistence that heavy industry be stripped of state support and allowed to perish may have been economically sound, but it led to intense protests and anger. The Scottish miners took great pride in their line of work and never forgave Thatcher for allowing the mining industry to collapse. Scottish anti-Thatcherism sentiments culminated in the 1984 Miners' Strike where mass protests led to violent confrontations between the Scottish miners and the police force. In 1989, another wave of protests occurred in response to the poll tax, which levied the same taxes on British citizens regardless of their income level. When prominent members of Thatcher's own party joined in the revolt, her political career came to an end. Thatcher's heavy-handed political style also helped to convince Scotland of the importance of having more control over its economic and political fate.

The average Scottish citizen may have been generally discontented with Westminster's decision-making, but British Prime Minister Edward Heath's decision to apply for a European Economic Community (EEC) membership in the 1970s had generally positive economic effects on Scotland. The EEC was the precursor of the European Union; it had been established on May 9, 1950, to promote transnational cooperation in the light of the disastrous losses incurred during World War II. Its aim was to promote peace, cooperation, and economic prosperity—it was in stark opposition to the climate of hostility and division engendered by the Cold War. Its six founding countries included Belgium, France, Germany, Italy, Luxembourg, and the Netherlands. The founding countries were not merely bound by lofty ideals; they also signed a treaty to operate their heavy industries (mainly coal and steel) under common management.[cxxxv] This would prevent any member nation from channeling its resources into war efforts against its allies. In 1957, the Treaty of Rome established the European common market, a then-radical economic agreement that allowed for people, goods, and services to move across borders without red tape and regulations.[cxxxvi]

In 1973, the United Kingdom joined the European Union alongside Denmark and Ireland. Scotland was a major beneficiary of the EU regional policy, which aimed to alleviate economic hardship in poorer areas by allocating large amounts of money to improve infrastructure and create job opportunities.[cxxxvii] Throughout the 70s,

Scotland received over twice the national average per capita via EU loans and grants Funds from the Coal and Steel Community, the European Social Fund, the European Investment Bank, and the European Regional Development Fund (ERDF) helped support local businesses, as well as allow Scotland to diversify its economy. Since it could no longer rely on its heavy industries, Scotland was encouraged to develop its financial services sector, tourism industry, cultural products, and biotechnology sector.

Despite the influx of foreign investments from the EU, the perception that Scotland was being economically short-changed by Westminster persisted. Many politicians and members of the public believed that the United Kingdom's policies were not tailored specifically to Scotland's unique challenges, leaving it at a disadvantage to London and southeastern England. The Scottish growth in national self-confidence and the belief that Scotland could—and should—govern itself led to the historic September 11, 1997, referendum where the Scottish population voted in favor of a devolved Parliament with the power to raise taxes.

The Scottish Parliament was thus established for the first time since the Act of Union in 1707. After the Conservatives lost all their Scottish seats, which were mainly swept up by the Labour Party, Prime Minister Tony Blair called for a referendum to assess the viability of reestablishing the Scottish Parliament. It would have control over Scotland's education and health care systems, and it was widely supported by the Liberal Democrats and the SNP. There were the expected growing pains, but the Scottish Parliament eventually evolved into a responsible legislative body that could defend Scottish national interests.

The growing thrust for Scottish independence and nationalism led to the unexpected SNP victory in the 2007 elections. After half a century of political dominance, the Labour Party was displaced from their majority position in the Scottish Parliament. SNP leader Alex Salmond became the first Nationalist to be elected First Minister of Scotland and went on to secure a second term in 2011.[cxxxviii] The following year, he secured the consent of British Prime Minister David Cameron to hold a referendum on Scotland's independence. Any Scottish citizen above the age of 16 was asked to answer a simple question on September 18, 2014: "Should Scotland be an independent country?"

Salmond argued that the union no longer served Scotland's national interests, especially since the discovery of oil and gas reserves in the North Sea could help finance its economic independence from England. Proceeds from the tax revenue for oil could be used to create a sovereign fund (similar to Norway's) which would protect the welfare of its citizens for generations. On the other hand, the Scottish government's desire to retain the pound through a formal currency union with the rest of the United Kingdom was a highly contentious issue.

In the end, it appeared that a majority of Scottish citizens were not ready for the idea of an independent Scotland. 3.6 million Scots (approximately 85% of registered voters) made the trip to the polling booths. 51% of those who voted preferred to remain a part of the United Kingdom, while 49% opted to cut ties with England, Wales, and Northern Ireland.

Despite this unfavorable outcome, the SNP won the election for the Scottish Parliament for a third time in May 2016. First Minister Nicola Sturgeon[cxxxix] was tasked with the difficult question of considering Scotland's next move in light of the United Kingdom's decision to leave the European Union (i.e., Brexit)[cxl] on June 23, 2016. A significant majority of Scottish voters had opted to remain in the EU (62%), but the overall majority across England, Northern Ireland, Wales, and Scotland opted to leave (51.9%). An age-old dilemma had reappeared in a modern setting: Should Scotland prioritize its ties to its southern neighbor or the wider European community at large?

As the Brexit negotiations intensify toward the United Kingdom's departure from the EU on October 31, 2019 (a deadline which has been extended from its previous date of March 29, 2019), Sturgeon's government appears to be intent on maintaining a strong economic and political alliance with the EU. It appears unlikely that Scotland will exit the UK in order to reapply for admission into the EU (this process could take years), so its best option is to maintain its position within the single market and customs union despite formally leaving the EU.[cxli] This would mean that Scotland would be able to export its goods to the rest of the EU without worrying about import taxes, embargoes, or levies, and that it would continue to adhere to the EU's uniform system for handling the flow of goods between member countries (no custom duties at borders between EU countries) and external nations (standard custom duties for goods from non-EU nations).[cxlii]

Conclusion

On August 3, 2018, *The Scotsman* journalist Joyce McMillan examined some of the findings from the Public Administration and Constitutional Affair's report on devolution and its impact on Britain's imminent withdrawal from the European Union.[cxliii] A clear conflict of interest between Westminster and Scotland emerges from this analysis. Under its EU Withdrawal Bill, the British government hopes to reclaim various legislative powers that were previously exercised at the EU level. The Scottish Parliament, however, is of the opinion that any powers that were not explicitly granted to Westminster should only be retained with the consent of the Scottish Parliament, as specified by the devolution model described in the Scotland Act of 1998.

The powers in question involve matters of broad national concerns, such as food safety laws, public service recruitment, and environmental laws. The Scottish Parliament is concerned that Westminster may compromise Scottish interests in its desperation to strike up a trade deal with United States President Donald Trump—a prospect that could easily materialize if Westminster can sideline the Scottish Parliament from the decision-making table. This situation also exemplifies the fact that the Westminster Parliament only holds its sovereignty as a matter of principle; the interest of the Scottish, the Welsh, and the Northern Irish are purely secondary.

As of April 2019, Scottish leaders are still waiting for Westminster to finalize the terms of the United Kingdom's impending exit from the European Union. Everything depends on the "hardness" or "softness" of this departure. A "hard" Brexit would mean sacrificing access to the single EU market in favor of full control over British borders. It would mean that British exports would be subjected to tariffs, and it would have to renegotiate all of its trade arrangements with foreign countries (e.g., the United States and Australia) which had previously signed trade agreements with the EU as a whole. A "soft" Brexit, on the other hand, would mean that the UK would retain access to the European single market (like Norway, Iceland, and Liechtenstein). It would also mean that the UK would have to allow the free flow of capital and labor through its borders.

Scottish First Minister Nicola Sturgeon has noted that her government "would—in good faith and a spirit of compromise— seek to identify a solution that might enable Scotland's voice to be heard, and mitigate the risks that Brexit poses to our interests within the UK."[cxliv] Sturgeon has pointed out that the majority of Scottish voters opted to remain in the EU and that access to the European single market was crucial. If Scotland cannot remain as a full member of the EU post-Brexit, then the option *may* be to seek full independence: "One option—in my view, the best option—is to become a full member of the EU as an independent country. Indeed, independence would resolve the fundamental cause of the position Scotland currently finds itself in: Westminster Governments that Scotland doesn't vote for, imposing policies that a majority in Scotland does not support."

This is undoubtedly the boldest of options, especially since the United Kingdom is a far more significant trade partner than the EU. In 2016, exports to the rest of the UK accounted for 61% (45.8 billion pounds) of total exports, while exports to the EU only accounted for 17% of total exports (12.7 billion pounds).[cxlv] Scotland's interests in maintaining ties with Europe is thus not purely materialistic. Sturgeon diplomatically contrasts the attractiveness of European ideals in contrast to Westminster's historical heavy-handedness in dealing with Scotland:

> Europe is about more than economics. The European ideal is one of peaceful co-existence, mutual solidarity and support, and prosperity built on co-operation. There is much still to achieve, but a Europe which encourages openness and civic dialogue, and which welcomes difference, is one from which

Scotland has gained much and to which it still wants to contribute.

Is history an endless cycle or a series of progressions and regressions? The dilemma that Sturgeon's government faces would certainly be familiar to many of Scotland's medieval kings, many of whom have actively sought fraternity with their counterparts in Europe as a means to neutralize the threat of their dominant southern neighbor. Sturgeon's emphasis on Europe welcoming "difference" hints at "inalienable rights" that the EU accords to its smaller members. Beneath its countless rules and treaties, there is an acceptance of cultural and historical differences between its members—a reflection of the post-World War II mentality that strives to avoid further conflicts between European nations. This acceptance of heterogeneity stands in contrast to the general pressure to conform and "Anglicize" according to English norms within the United Kingdom. The pragmatic benefits of a continued relationship with England and the United Kingdom as a whole remain, but this relationship is predicated on Scottish interests playing second fiddle to Westminster's.

Sturgeon herself has made it clear that she wishes for Scotland to finally wrestle its right to complete autonomy—a desire to be free of Westminster—once and for all.[cxlvi] Her patience indicates that she has a long-term strategy in mind. After calling for a second referendum in 2016 (after Brexit), which Theresa May denied, she obtained a good sense of Scotland's appetite for independence in the light of an impending loss of EU membership. In the meantime, Scotland looks inward toward its various problems—social and economic inequalities, divisions between the Catholics and Protestants, and its economic prospects in the near future—before contemplating its place in a politically volatile world. These challenges may appear novel, but they have nearly always been a part of Scotland's unique history. After all these years, the questions of rights, sovereignty, and economic necessity are as pertinent as ever.

Here's another book by Captivating History that we think you'd be interested in

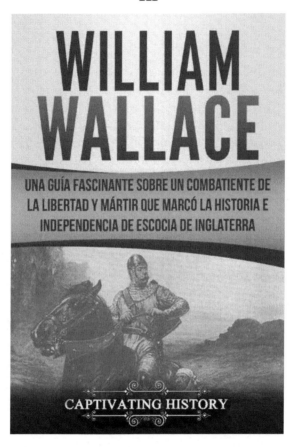

And another one...

WARS OF SCOTTISH INDEPENDENCE

A CAPTIVATING GUIDE TO THE BATTLES BETWEEN
THE KINGDOM OF SCOTLAND AND THE KINGDOM OF ENGLAND,
INCLUDING THE IMPACT MADE BY KING ROBERT THE BRUCE

CAPTIVATING HISTORY

References

[i] "10 things you (probably) didn't know about Scottish history." *History Extra*. https://www.historyextra.com/period/prehistoric/10-things-you-probably-didnt-know-about-scottish-history/. Accessed 15 July 2018.

[ii] Wormald, Jenny. *Scotland: A History*. 2005.

[iii] "Scotland: Constituent of United Kingdom." *Encyclopedia Britannica*. https://www.britannica.com/place/Scotland. Accessed 15 July 2018.

[iv] Wormald, Jenny. *Scotland: A History*. 2005.

[v] "Climate change." *Encyclopedia Britannica*. https://www.britannica.com/science/climate-change. Accessed 15 July 2018.

[vi] "Ancient Rome." *Encyclopedia Britannica*. https://www.britannica.com/place/ancient-Rome. Accessed 15 July 2018.

[vii] Wormald, Jenny. *Scotland: A History*. 2005.

[viii] "Roman Timeline of the 1st Century AD." *United Nations of Roma Victrix (UNRV)*. https://www.unrv.com/empire/timeline-of-first-century.php. Accessed 15 July 2018.

[ix] "Hadrian's Wall." *Encyclopedia Britannica*. https://www.britannica.com/topic/Hadrians-Wall. Accessed 15 July 2018.

[x] "Antoine Wall." *Encyclopedia Britannica.*
https://www.britannica.com/topic/Antonine-Wall. Accessed 15 July
2018.

[xi] "Briton people." *Encyclopedia Britannica.*
https://www.britannica.com/topic/Briton. Accessed 15 July 2018.

[xii] "Pict people." *Encyclopedia Britannica.*
https://www.britannica.com/topic/Pict. Accessed 15 July 2018.

[xiii] "Scot: ancient people." *Encyclopedia Britannica.*
https://www.britannica.com/topic/Scot. Accessed 15 July 2018.

[xiv] "Angle people." *Encyclopedia Britannica.*
https://www.britannica.com/topic/Angle-people. Accessed 15 July
2018.

[xv] "The truth about the Picts." *The Independent.*
https://www.independent.co.uk/news/science/the-truth-about-the-
picts-886098.html. Accessed 15 July 2018.

[xvi] "Scots Gaelic language." *Encyclopedia Britannica.*
https://www.britannica.com/topic/Scots-Gaelic-language. Accessed
15 July 2018.

[xvii] "Dalriada." *Encyclopedia Britannica.*
https://www.britannica.com/place/Dalriada. Accessed 15 July 2018.

[xviii] "Saint Columba." *Encyclopedia Britannica.*
https://www.britannica.com/biography/Saint-Columba. Accessed 15
July 2018.

[xix] "Iona." *Encyclopedia Britannica.*
https://www.britannica.com/place/Iona-island-Inner-Hebrides-
Scotland. Accessed 15 July 2018.

[xx] "Viking People." *Encyclopedia Britannica.*
https://www.britannica.com/topic/Viking-people. Accessed 15 July
2018.

[xxi] "Kenneth I." *Encyclopedia Britannica.*
https://www.britannica.com/biography/Kenneth-I. Accessed 15 July

2018.

[xxii] "Kenneth MacAlpin." *BBC.*
http://www.bbc.co.uk/scotland/history/articles/kenneth_macalpin/.
Accessed 15 July 2018.

[xxiii] "Alba." *Encyclopedia Britannica.*
https://www.britannica.com/place/Alba-historical-kingdom-
Scotland. Accessed 15 July 2018.

[xxiv] "William Shakespeare." *Encyclopedia Britannica.*
https://www.britannica.com/biography/William-Shakespeare.
Accessed 15 July 2018.

[xxv] "Macbeth: Work by Shakespeare." *Encyclopedia Britannica.*
https://www.britannica.com/topic/Macbeth-by-Shakespeare.
Accessed 15 July 2018.

[xxvi] "Macbeth: King of Scots." *Encyclopedia Britannica.*
https://www.britannica.com/biography/Macbeth-king-of-Scots.
Accessed 15 July 2018.

[xxvii] "Duncan and MacBeth." *Historic UK.* https://www.historic-
uk.com/HistoryUK/HistoryofScotland/Duncan-MacBeth/. Accessed
15 July 2018.

[xxviii] "Duncan I." *Encyclopedia Britannica.*
https://www.britannica.com/biography/Duncan-I. Accessed 15 July
2018.

[xxix] "Malcolm II." *Encyclopedia Britannica.*
https://www.britannica.com/biography/Malcolm-II. Accessed 15
July 2018.

[xxx] "Macbeth." *BBC.*
http://www.bbc.co.uk/history/historic_figures/macbeth.shtml.
Accessed 15 July 2018.

[xxxi] "Malcolm III Canmore." *Encyclopedia Britannica.*
https://www.britannica.com/biography/Malcolm-III-Canmore.
Accessed 15 July 2018.

xxxii "Tanistry." *Encyclopedia Britannica.* https://www.britannica.com/topic/tanistry. Accessed 15 July 2018.

xxxiii Smith, Julia M.H. *Europe after Rome: A New Cultural History 500-1000.* 2007

xxxiv "Saint Margaret." *Encyclopedia Britannica.* https://www.britannica.com/biography/Saint-Margaret-of-Scotland. Accessed 15 July 2018.

xxxv "Primogeniture and ultimogeniture." *Encyclopedia Britannica.* https://www.britannica.com/topic/primogeniture. Accessed 15 July 2018.

xxxvi "David I: King of Scotland." *Encyclopedia Britannica.* https://www.britannica.com/biography/David-I. Accessed 15 July 2018.

xxxvii "David I and the impact of the Norman Conquest." *BBC.* http://www.bbc.co.uk/legacies/immig_emig/scotland/borders/article_1.shtml. Accessed 15 July 2018.

xxxviii "Anglo Norman." *Encyclopedia Britannica.* https://www.britannica.com/topic/Anglo-Norman-people. Accessed 15 July 2018.

xxxix "David I." *Oxford Dictionary of National Biography.* http://www.oxforddnb.com/view/10.1093/ref:odnb/9780198614128.001.0001/odnb-9780198614128-e-7208. Accessed 15 July 2018.

xl "Feudalism." *Encyclopedia Britannica.* https://www.britannica.com/topic/feudalism. Accessed 15 July 2018.

xli Wormald, Jenny. *Scotland: A History.* 2005.

xlii "Malcolm IV." *Encyclopedia Britannica.* https://www.britannica.com/biography/Malcolm-IV. Accessed 15 July 2018.

xliii Wormald, Jenny. *Scotland: A History.* 2005.

[xliv] "Berwick." *Encyclopedia Britannica.*
https://www.britannica.com/place/Berwickshire. Accessed 15 June 2018.

[xlv] "Glasgow." *Encyclopedia Britannica.*
https://www.britannica.com/place/Glasgow-Scotland. Accessed 15 June 2018.

[xlvi] "Edinburgh." *Encyclopedia Britannica.*
https://www.britannica.com/place/Edinburgh-Scotland. Accessed 15 June 2018.

[xlvii] "The Lords of the Isles." *BBC.*
http://www.bbc.co.uk/scotland/history/articles/lords_of_the_isles/. Accessed 15 June 2018.

[xlviii] "William I: King of Scotland." *Encyclopedia Britannica.*
https://www.britannica.com/biography/William-I-king-of-Scotland. Accessed 15 July 2018.

[xlix] "Alexander II: King of Scotland." *Encyclopedia Britannica.*
https://www.britannica.com/biography/Alexander-II-king-of-Scotland. Accessed 15 July 2018.

[l] "Alexander III: King of Scotland." *Encyclopedia Britannica.*
https://www.britannica.com/biography/Alexander-III-king-of-Scotland. Accessed 15 July 2018.

[li] "The last battle of the Vikings." *BBC.*
https://www.bbc.com/news/uk-scotland-20697117. Accessed 15 July 2018.

[lii] "Haakon IV Haakonsson: King of Norway." *Encyclopedia Britannica.* https://www.britannica.com/biography/Haakon-IV-Haakonsson. Accessed 15 July 2018.

[liii] "Margaret: Queen of Scotland." *Encyclopedia Britannica.*
https://www.britannica.com/biography/Margaret-queen-of-Scotland. Accessed 15 July 2018.

liv "The Treaty of Birgham." *BBC.*
http://www.bbc.co.uk/bitesize/higher/history/warsofindependence/th
egreatcause/revision/2/. Accessed 15 July 2018.

lv "John de Balliol: Scottish magnate." *Encyclopedia Britannica.*
https://www.britannica.com/biography/John-de-Balliol. Accessed 15
July 2018.

lvi "Robert de Bruce: King of Scotland." *Encyclopedia Britannica.*
https://www.britannica.com/biography/Robert-the-Bruce. Accessed
15 July 2018.

lvii "William Wallace." *BBC.*
http://www.bbc.co.uk/scotland/history/articles/william_wallace/.
Accessed 15 July 2018.

lviii "Battle of Falkirk." *Encyclopedia Britannica.*
https://www.britannica.com/topic/battle-of-Falkirk. Accessed 15
March 2018.

lix "Robert the Bruce, King of Scots 1306 – 1329." *BBC.*
http://www.bbc.co.uk/scotland/history/articles/robert_the_bruce/.
Accessed 15 July 2018.

lx "War of Independence." *BBC.*
http://www.bbc.co.uk/scotland/education/as/warsofindependence/inf
o.shtml?loc=stone. Accessed 15 July 2018.

lxi "The rise and triumph of Robert Bruce." *BBC.*
https://www.bbc.com/bitesize/guides/zptthyc/revision/4. Accessed
17 August 2018.

lxii "Battle of Bannockburn." *Encyclopedia Britannica.*
https://www.britannica.com/event/Battle-of-Bannockburn. Accessed
15 July 2018.

lxiii "Treaty of Northampton." *Encyclopedia Britannica.*
https://www.britannica.com/topic/Treaty-of-Northampton. Accessed
15 July 2018.

[lxiv] "Harry the Minstrel: Scottish writer." *Encyclopedia Britannica.* https://www.britannica.com/biography/Harry-the-Minstrel. Accessed 15 July 2018.

[lxv] "Braveheart: Film by Gibson [1995]." *Encyclopedia Britannica.* https://www.britannica.com/topic/Braveheart. Accessed 15 July 2018.

[lxvi] "John Barbour." *Encyclopedia Britannica.* https://www.britannica.com/biography/John-Barbour. Accessed 15 July 2018.

[lxvii] "Black Death." *Encyclopedia Britannica.* https://www.britannica.com/event/Black-Death. Accessed 15 July 2018.

[lxviii] Ormrod, W. M. and Phillip Lindley. *The Black Death in England.* 2003.

[lxix] "Scotland Back in the Day: Black Death changed the country forever". *The National.* http://www.thenational.scot/culture/14864611.Scotland_Back_in_the_Day__Black_Death_changed_the_country_forever/. Accessed 15 July 2018.

[lxx] "David II: King of Scotland." *Encyclopedia Britannica.* https://www.britannica.com/biography/David-II. Accessed 15 July 2018.

[lxxi] "House of Stuart." *Encyclopedia Britannica.* https://www.britannica.com/topic/House-of-Stuart. Accessed 15 July 2018.

[lxxii] "Robert II: King of Scotland." *Encyclopedia Britannica.* https://www.britannica.com/biography/Robert-II-king-of-Scotland. Accessed 15 July 2018.

[lxxiii]"Robert III: King of Scotland." *Encyclopedia Britannica.* https://www.britannica.com/biography/Robert-III. Accessed 15 July 2018.

lxxiv "James I: King of Scotland." *Encyclopedia Britannica.* https://www.britannica.com/biography/James-I-king-of-Scotland. Accessed 15 July 2018.

lxxv "James II: King of Scotland." *Encyclopedia Britannica.* https://www.britannica.com/biography/James-II-king-of-Scotland. Accessed 15 July 2018.

lxxvi "James III: King of Scotland." *Encyclopedia Britannica.* https://www.britannica.com/biography/James-III-king-of-Scotland. Accessed 15 July 2018.

lxxvii "Benedict (XIII): Antipope." *Encyclopedia Britannica.* https://www.britannica.com/biography/Benedict-XIII-antipope. Accessed 20 August 2018.

lxxviii "Western Schism." *Encyclopedia Britannica.* https://www.britannica.com/event/Western-Schism. Accessed 20 August 2018.

lxxix "University of Glasgow." *Encyclopedia Britannica.* https://www.britannica.com/topic/University-of-Glasgow. Accessed 15 July 2018.

lxxx "James IV: King of Scotland." *Encyclopedia Britannica.* https://www.britannica.com/biography/James-IV-king-of-Scotland. Accessed 15 July 2018.

lxxxi "Italian Wars." *Encyclopedia Britannica.* https://www.britannica.com/event/Italian-Wars.

lxxxii "James V: King of Scotland." *Encyclopedia Britannica.* https://www.britannica.com/biography/James-V. Accessed 15 July 2018.

lxxxiii "Mary: Queen of Scotland." *Encyclopedia Britannica.* https://www.britannica.com/biography/Mary-queen-of-Scotland. Accessed 15 July 2018.

lxxxiv "Mary of Lorraine." *Encyclopedia Britannica.* https://www.britannica.com/biography/Mary-of-Lorraine. Accessed 15 July 2018.

lxxxv "Mary, Queen of Scots." *BBC.* http://www.bbc.co.uk/history/people/mary_queen_of_scots/. Accessed 15 July 2018.

lxxxvi "Francis II: King of France." *Encyclopedia Britannica.* https://www.britannica.com/biography/Francis-II-king-of-France. Accessed 15 July 2018.

lxxxvii "Elizabeth I: Queen of England." *Encyclopedia Britannica.* https://www.britannica.com/biography/Elizabeth-I. Accessed 15 July 2018.

lxxxviii"James Stewart, 1st earl of Moray." *Encyclopedia Britannica.* https://www.britannica.com/biography/James-Stewart-1st-Earl-of-Moray. Accessed 15 July 2018.

lxxxix"Henry Stewart, Lord Darnley." *Encyclopedia Britannica.* https://www.britannica.com/biography/Henry-Stewart-Lord-Darnley. Accessed 15 July 2018.

xc "David Riccio." *Encyclopedia Britannica.* https://www.britannica.com/biography/David-Riccio. Accessed 15 July 2018.

xci"James Hepburn, 4th earl of Bothwell." *Encyclopedia Britannica.* https://www.britannica.com/biography/James-Hepburn-4th-Earl-of-Bothwell. Accessed 15 July 2018.

xcii "James I: King of England and Scotland." *Encyclopedia Britannica.* https://www.britannica.com/biography/James-I-king-of-England-and-Scotland. Accessed 15 July 2018.

xciii "Anne of Denmark." *Encyclopedia Britannica.* https://www.britannica.com/biography/Anne-of-Denmark. Accessed 15 July 2018.

[xciv] "Reformed and Presbyterian churches." *Encyclopedia Britannica.* https://www.britannica.com/topic/Presbyterian-churches. Accessed 15 July 2018.

[xcv] "George Buchanan." *Encyclopedia Britannica.* https://www.britannica.com/biography/George-Buchanan. Accessed 15 July 2018.

[xcvi] "King James Version." *Encyclopedia Britannica.* https://www.britannica.com/topic/King-James-Version. Accessed 15 July 2018.

[xcvii] "Divine right of kings." *Encyclopedia Britannica.* https://www.britannica.com/topic/divine-right-of-kings. Accessed 15 July 2018.

[xcviii] "Charles I: King of Great Britain and Ireland." *Encyclopedia Britannica.* https://www.britannica.com/biography/Charles-I-king-of-Great-Britain-and-Ireland. Accessed 15 July 2018.

[xcix] "Act of Union." *Encyclopedia Britannica.* https://www.britannica.com/event/Act-of-Union-Great-Britain-1707. Accessed 15 July 2018.

[c] "Oliver Cromwell." *Encyclopedia Britannica.* https://www.britannica.com/biography/Oliver-Cromwell. Accessed 15 July 2018.

[ci] "James II: King of Great Britain." *Encyclopedia Britannica.* https://www.britannica.com/biography/James-II-king-of-Great-Britain. Accessed 15 July 2018.

[cii] "William III: King of England, Scotland and Ireland." *Encyclopedia Britannica.* https://www.britannica.com/biography/William-III-king-of-England-Scotland-and-Ireland. Accessed 15 July 2018.

[ciii] "Act of Union 1707." *Parliament UK.* https://www.parliament.uk/about/living-heritage/evolutionofparliament/legislativescrutiny/act-of-union-1707/. Accessed 15 July 2018.

civ "The Scottish Enlightenment." *Encyclopedia Britannica.* https://www.britannica.com/topic/Scottish-Enlightenment. Accessed 15 July 2018.

cv "David Hume." *Encyclopedia Britannica.* https://www.britannica.com/biography/David-Hume. Accessed 17 August 2018.

cvi "Adam Smith." *Encyclopedia Britannica.* https://www.britannica.com/biography/Adam-Smith. Accessed 17 August 2018.

cvii "James Hutton." *Encyclopedia Britannica.* https://www.britannica.com/biography/James-Hutton. Accessed 15 July 2018.

cviii "Industrial revolution." *Encyclopedia Britannica.* https://www.britannica.com/event/Industrial-Revolution. Accessed 15 July 2018.

cix "Great Famine." *Encyclopedia Britannica.* https://www.britannica.com/event/Great-Famine-Irish-history. Accessed 15 July 2018.

cx "The Enlightenment and Industrial Revolution." *BBC.* https://www.bbc.co.uk/history/scottishhistory/enlightenment/features_enlightenment_industry.shtml. Accessed 15 July 2018.

cxi "The Rise of Glasgow: Urban Growth in Victorian Scotland." *BBC.* https://www.bbc.co.uk/history/scottishhistory/victorian/features_victorian_urban.shtml. Accessed 17 August 2018.

cxii "Impact on the Countryside." *BBC.* https://www.bbc.co.uk/history/scottishhistory/victorian/features_victorian_railways3.shtml. Accessed 17 August 2018.

cxiii "Transatlantic slave trade." *Encyclopedia Britannica.* https://www.britannica.com/topic/transatlantic-slave-trade. Accessed 15 July 2018.

[cxiv] "World War I." *Encyclopedia Britannica.* https://www.britannica.com/event/World-War-I. Accessed 15 July 2018.

[cxv] "World War II." *Encyclopedia Britannica.* https://www.britannica.com/event/World-War-II. Accessed 15 July 2018.

[cxvi] "Scotland & World War II." *Travel Scotland.* https://www.scotland.org.uk/history/second-worldwar. Accessed 17 August 2018.

[cxvii] "20th Century Scottish Women - Changing Roles." *BBC.* https://www.bbc.co.uk/history/scottishhistory/modern/features_mod ern_women.shtml. Accessed 17 August 2018.

[cxviii] "Women's rights and suffragettes." *Scotland's History.* http://www.sath.org.uk/edscot/www.educationscotland.gov.uk/scotla ndshistory/20thand21stcenturies/womensrights/index.html. Accessed 17 August 2018.

[cxix] "Five landmark moments from Scotland's struggle for women's suffrage." *The Scotsman.* https://www.scotsman.com/news/five-landmark-moments-from-scotland-s-struggle-for-women-s-suffrage-1-4684266. Accessed 17 August 2018.

[cxx] "Marie Stopes." *Encyclopedia Britannica.* https://www.britannica.com/biography/Marie-Stopes. Accessed 17 August 2018.

[cxxi] "Nicola Sturgeon." *Encyclopedia Britannica.* https://www.britannica.com/biography/Nicola-Sturgeon. Accessed 17 August 2018.

[cxxii] "Timeline: gay rights." *The Guardian.* https://www.theguardian.com/politics/2003/jun/30/immigrationpolic y.gayrights1. Accessed 17 August 2018.

[cxxiii] "Wolfenden Report." *Encyclopedia Britannica.* https://www.britannica.com/event/Wolfenden-Report. Accessed 17 August 2018.

[cxxiv] "Illegal to be gay - Scotland's history." *BBC.* https://www.bbc.com/news/uk-scotland-40731733. Accessed 17 August 2018.

[cxxv] "Policy: LGBTI." *Scottish Government.* https://beta.gov.scot/policies/lgbti/. Accessed 17 August 2018.

[cxxvi] "Scotland tops league for gay rights." *The Guardian.* https://www.theguardian.com/world/2015/may/10/scotland-tops-league-for-gay-rights. Accessed 17 August 2018.

[cxxvii] "How Scotland Became the Most LGBT Friendly Country in the World." *Vice.* https://www.vice.com/en_us/article/vdxw93/scottish-politics-lgbt-leadership. Accessed 17 August 2018.

[cxxviii] "Scotland is no longer the 'best place in Europe' on LGBT rights." *Pink News.* https://www.pinknews.co.uk/2017/05/17/scotland-is-no-longer-the-best-place-in-europe-on-lgbt-rights/. Accessed 17 August 2018.

[cxxix] "Loch Ness monster." *Encyclopedia Britannica.* https://www.britannica.com/topic/Loch-Ness-monster-legendary-creature. Accessed 17 August 2018.

[cxxx] "How scientists debunked the Loch Ness Monster." *Vox.* https://www.vox.com/2015/4/21/8459353/loch-ness-monster. Accessed 17 August 2018.

[cxxxi] "What happens if someone catches the Loch Ness Monster?" *BBC.* https://www.bbc.com/news/uk-scotland-highlands-islands-44519189. Accessed 17 August 2018.

[cxxxii] "Mythical Scotland: Exploring the Legends." *Nordic Visitor.* https://www.nordicvisitor.com/blog/mythical-scotland-exploring-the-legends/. Accessed 17 August 2018.

[cxxxiii] "Scotland: Cultural life." *Encyclopedia Britannica.* https://www.britannica.com/place/Scotland/Cultural-life#ref44608. Accessed 15 July 2018.

cxxxiv "Margaret Thatcher." *Encyclopedia Britannica.* https://www.britannica.com/biography/Margaret-Thatcher. Accessed 15 July 2018.

cxxxv "The EU in brief." *Europa.* https://europa.eu/european-union/about-eu/eu-in-brief_en#from-economic-to-political-union. Accessed 17 August 2018.

cxxxvi "A peaceful Europe – the beginnings of cooperation." *Europa.* https://europa.eu/european-union/about-eu/history/1945-1959_en. Accessed 17 August 2018.

cxxxvii "The history of the European Union." *Europa.* https://europa.eu/european-union/about-eu/history_en. Accessed 17 August 2018.

cxxxviii "Alex Salmond." *Encyclopedia Britannica.* https://www.britannica.com/biography/Alex-Salmond. Accessed 15 July 2018.

cxxxix "Nicola Sturgeon." *Encyclopedia Britannica.* https://www.britannica.com/biography/Nicola-Sturgeon. Accessed 15 July 2018.

cxl "Brexit: The U.K. Votes to Exit the EU." *Encyclopedia Britannica.* https://www.britannica.com/topic/Brexit-The-U-K-Votes-to-Exit-the-EU-2075293. Accessed 15 July 2018.

cxli "European Union." *Encyclopedia Britannica.* https://www.britannica.com/topic/European-Union. Accessed 15 July 2018.

cxlii "EU Customs Union – unique in the world." *European Commission.* https://ec.europa.eu/taxation_customs/facts-figures/eu-customs-union-unique-world_en. Accessed 17 August 2018.

cxliii "Joyce McMillan: Is Scotland the real 'vassal' state? *The Scotsman.* https://www.scotsman.com/news/opinion/joyce-mcmillan-is-scotland-the-real-vassal-state-1-4777919. Accessed 5 August 2018.

[cxliv] "Scotland's place in Europe." *Scottish Government.* https://beta.gov.scot/publications/scotlands-place-europe/. Accessed 15 July 2018.

[cxlv] "Export statistics Scotland 2016." *Scottish Government.* https://www.gov.scot/Topics/Statistics/Browse/Economy/Exports/ESSPublication. Accessed 15 July 2018.

[cxlvi] "Sturgeon is preparing for a new Scottish independence battle." *The Guardian.* https://www.theguardian.com/commentisfree/2018/jul/01/nicola-sturgeon-preparing-scottish-independence-battle. Accessed 15 July 2018.

Made in the USA
Lexington, KY
14 May 2019